D1623831

The Essential Advisor

The Essential Advisor

Building Value in the
Investor-Advisor Relationship

Bill Crager
Jay Hummel

WILEY

To our families, colleagues, clients, and friends who make us better every day

Contents

Foreword

On January 6, 2016, the day Bill Crager and Jay Hummel asked me to write the foreword for this book, the Dow marked its worst four-day start to a year on record. Crude oil sank to a seven-year low. And that was just the bumpy beginning of a tumultuous month—a month marked by headlines with words like: *Plunge. Bear. Wild.* Even *Ouch* (kudos, CNN.com). It was a month when I found myself on the air repeating the same mantra over and over: *I know it's hard, but try to be calm. As long as you're in it for the long term, do your best to stick to your plan.*

Still, you couldn't blame even seasoned investors for their frazzled nerves. The stakes Americans have in securing their own comfortable financial futures have never been higher. We are responsible for our own finances to a degree that earlier generations never imagined. The pensions that were there for our grandparents (and a few of our parents) are largely gone, replaced by 401(k)s and other defined contribution accounts that we have to fund and manage ourselves. Employer-sponsored health care is fading quickly. In 2007, nearly three-quarters of employers were certain they'd still be offering an employer plan a decade down the road, according to Towers Watson. By 2014, just one-quarter felt the same way. As for Social Security, pundits may believe it's here for the long term; individuals not so much. According to AARP, 57 percent of people are not confident in the future of the program (unfortunate, since 80 percent say they'll rely on it for income).

The extra financial responsibility we're being asked to shoulder wouldn't be as much of a problem if it came with an instruction manual. It doesn't. In 2016, only 20 states require high school students to take a course in economics, according to the Council for Economic Education—that's two fewer than had the requirement in 2014. Just 17 states mandate personal finance. It would be nice to think that parents could simply pass their financial smarts onto their own children. That's not happening in a world where 40 percent of Americans consistently give themselves a grade of C, D, or F when it comes to their personal finances, according to the annual Consumer Financial Literacy

Survey. Is it any wonder that the leading cause of stress among American adults is—you guessed it—money?

I like to tell people I've had a ringside seat at the personal finance revolution. For the past two and a half decades—from my perches at *Forbes*, SmartMoney, *Money*, and the *Today* show—I've chronicled how Americans make their money, save it, spend it, invest it, and protect it. I've examined not just the technical side of personal finance, but the behavioral and emotional components, repeatedly asking: Why do we do things with our money we know are not in our own best interest? More importantly, how do we stop?

Advice—good advice, holistic advice—is a big part of the answer.

To understand why, think about three facts of modern life. One: We are starved for time. Working Americans (particularly those who are either working parents or—like many of your clients—have demanding jobs, or both) will tell you they don't have time to do the things they want. And when they choose how to allocate their limited time off, there are a whole bunch of line items that rank a lot higher than rebalancing their portfolios. Two: The immediate gratification itch that lords over everything from how we shop (ahem, Amazon Prime) to how we watch our favorite shows (cough, Roku) plays a role in our finances, too. We don't come for financial advice just because. We seek it because we have an issue—we're getting married, having a baby, turning 50, getting divorced—and then we don't just need help, we need it *now*. And three: The financial landscape is getting more complicated every year. It's not just that there are thousands of investments (8,000-plus mutual funds, 1,600-plus ETFs) to choose from. It's that the problems we are being asked to solve have multiplied. For years, personal finance publications preached one main thing: Grow your nest egg. Now we have to turn the puzzle on its head and make the money last.

Unfortunately, all of those things stand squarely in the way of doing a good job with your money. Surveys that show Americans are spending more time planning a vacation than retirement, or that we'd rather go to the dentist than spend an equal amount of time learning about money may have been fielded to garner splashy headlines. But they make a point. On the whole, many of us don't put the time we should into our finances. And when we do turn to our money, it's often in the wrong frame of mind—because we've had an emergency or because the markets are down big. When we're emotional, we're not rational, particularly where large sums of money are concerned. That makes it especially difficult to wrap your brain around issues where there are no right answers to complex questions: How long *are* you going to live? How long *will* you be able to work? How much money *will* you actually need year in and year out?

Enter *The Essential Advisor.* As you read the book Bill and Jay have thoughtfully put together, you'll understand why I believe financial advisors have never been more important—and why I believe advice is worth paying for. There's no question that there are plenty of tools available for DIY investors; many of them are excellent. What is in doubt is how many people will actually use those tools. Your portfolio is no different from your lawn in that regard. If you're not going to mow it yourself, it still has to be done. Paying someone to do it for you is much saner than letting the grass become an eyesore. In the case of your portfolio, it also happens to be profitable. ROA—or Return On Advice—is something you can quantify.

Envestnet's study of ROA (tested on thousands of advisors) shows advisors have the potential to add 3 percent in value to their clients annually. Some of the added value comes from investment selection and asset allocation, some from systematic rebalancing and targeted tax management. But I believe the biggest benefit comes from simply having a plan designed to help you get from where you are today to where you want to go tomorrow—and a trusted advisor on your team to help you stay on course.

Which brings me back to January 2016. As I blogged and tweeted and reported on the ongoing rollercoaster in the markets, I took the time to check in with my own financial advisor. Many people are surprised to hear that I have one. But I have for years, for the same reasons I believe others should, and it's a relationship I value tremendously. I shot off a quick e-mail with the subject line: *Yikes.* "I guess after a six-year bull market this is what we get. Anything special you're doing over there?" The return came back in momentarily. "Meeting/talking with lots of clients, and never fun, but fundamentally staying the course, as usual." He signed off with a promise that I'd receive a call shortly.

Then I did.

Jean Chatzky
February 2016

Preface

Naming a book is more challenging than one would think. Our goal in picking the title was to make our point of view perfectly clear: we believe the advisor is *essential* now and into the future in helping more consumers reach their goals and achieve their dreams. Consumers need more advice, not less. This book will most likely be read by advisors who want to continue making themselves essential to delivering better outcomes for their current and prospective clients. However, we believe consumers will benefit from reading it because we also focus on understanding what advisors do, how they deliver better results for consumers, and how consumers should think about the industry and selecting an advisor.

We have day jobs, and understanding what we do in them is important to understanding the approach for this book and our perspectives. Bill is the cofounder and president of Envestnet and Jay is the managing director of Strategic Initiatives and Thought Leadership at Envestnet, where he focuses on advisor training, innovation, and consulting. Envestnet was founded to provide end-to-end technology and consulting solutions to independent financial advisors. At Envestnet, we are solely focused on helping advisors and financial institutions bring better outcomes and financial wellness to their clients. At a time when some are questioning whether financial advisors will be relevant 10 years from now, we believe they will not only be relevant, but more relevant than they are today. Advisors change lives. Investable assets aren't numbers on a page. Investable assets are deferred spending accounts. Investing is an action of trust and hope—trusting the assets will someday be used for something good. When an investor spends their savings to attain a goal, that's where joy happens. This goal may be retirement, a vacation, taking care of a loved one, or sending a child to their dream college. Better financial advice means better lives.

When we talked to our friend Rob Densen, founder of the advocacy marketing company Tiller, about the book, he cautioned us to make sure we don't look like "homers" . . . a sports reference for a fan that roots for their home team so passionately that the team can do no wrong. The fans are blinded from reality by their passion. He cautioned us not to do the same for our industry, our company, and advisors in general. His point was a good one. Others cautioned us not to do it at all, not to have strong opinions about the industry. We serve more than 42,000 advisors today and there's some potential risk in us writing this book because, in some ways, we are critical of some aspects of the industry and how it's been built. As an industry, we aren't perfect. As a company, we aren't perfect. The advisory community isn't perfect. Nobody expects anyone to be so. We hope this book provides a view forward to an evolving industry and serves as a driving force for all of us to continue to push ourselves to become better for our clients.

As a backup to ensure the reader also knows our opinions are independent, we are lucky to have Pam Krueger partnering with us on this effort. We know advisors. We know how they operate and how they should for the future. However, until recently, as a company and as people, we've spent little time thinking about the end investor. As a Gracie Award–winning host of the Emmy Award–winning PBS show *MoneyTrack*, which focused on helping end consumers make better financial decisions, Pam has listened to thousands of consumers. She kept us honest in this effort by helping us to view our industry through the lens of those we are trying to attract to it, as clients and future generations of financial services leaders. You will see a consumer perspective section at the end of each chapter. We believe this effort will not only provide an important voice, but also help achieve a goal of the book: to bring the consumers and advisors closer together.

Although we sit on the same side of the table as the financial advisors and enterprises we serve, as a company we pride ourselves on being independent. We understand there are a lot of different models out there to deliver advice. Some models are arguably better than others, but as long as the consumer is getting nonconflicted advice, then we believe our industry has achieved its purpose.

When we set out on the journey to write this book, we had three objectives: have fun, write something that adds to the industry conversation in a constructive way, and bring the consumer and advisor closer together without being too academic or preachy. We certainly had fun in this effort. Whether we achieved our other two goals is for the readers to decide. We hope we meet your needs. Enjoy the book.

Bill Crager and Jay Hummel

Acknowledgments

We are both avid sports fans. Writing a book is a lot like being an athlete on a team. The athletes on the field tend to get most or all of the credit even though there are dozens of people supporting the victories. Our names are on the cover and we will get a lot of credit for what we hope the readers consider was a victory. However, this was a huge team effort. First and foremost, thanks to three key collaborators in this effort: Jean Chatzky, Les Abromovitz, and Pam Krueger. Jean wrote an outstanding Foreword and is the type of financial advocate the investing population needs in this world. Les drafted and edited much of this book, making the ideas that always sounded good in our heads sound much better on paper. Pam brought her consumer insights to the book, helping us meet our goal of bridging the advisor and consumer gap. We believe her consumer perspectives throughout this effort will prove to be invaluable to the reader. We are indebted to the three of you for your efforts. A special thanks also to those who subjected themselves to our probing questions through their interviews. Please see the biographies of the outstanding individuals who agreed to do interviews and be included in this effort in the back of the book. We are honored you came along for the ride.

We want to thank our families who support our crazy schedules and all that we do. Our wives, Kathy and Valerie, are outstanding partners. Our kids help us stay focused on what really matters in life.

We are lucky to have outstanding colleagues at Envestnet. We have over 2,000 employees who work tirelessly each and every day to help our clients achieve their goals and remain focused on the audacious goal of not only being the best company *in* the financial services industry, but the best *for* the industry. We hope our colleagues believe our efforts here are as excellent as their teamwork. Some colleagues went above and beyond to support this effort. We owe a big thank you to Karen Lanzetta, Cindy Siegel, and Jaime Hernandez. Thanks to our CEO and friend, Jud Bergman, for writing an outstanding strategic piece you will find at the end of the book in a section entitled "The Last

Word." His strategic vision herein and at our company is contagious. Thanks to Rob Densen and "Team Tiller" for coming up with the title of the book.

Lastly, thanks to our amazing clients who give us the opportunity to serve them and gain insights about their businesses, which served as the foundation of this book. Without you, this book would not exist. We look forward to building many success stories and memories with you in the times ahead.

CHAPTER 1

The Evolution of Financial Advice

You can't connect the dots looking forward; you can only connect them looking backwards. So you have to trust that the dots will somehow connect in your future.

—Steve Jobs

Advice is essential for people to reach their financial goals and dreams. Technology has made it so much easier for consumers to access information, and it is important for advisors to recognize how this impacts their role—for better and for worse. As consumers think about their changing demands, and as advisors position themselves for the future, both groups must understand how drastically the financial system has evolved. It's easy to forget that not long ago the financial landscape was very different. For example, we take for granted the number of transactions we can handle on our phones. Even 10 years ago the thought of moving money with the swipe of a finger or depositing a check by taking a picture seemed crazy.

In the broad history of our industry, the 1950s wasn't that long ago. During that time, when consumers had a few dollars to put away, they opened a savings account. At some savings and loans (S&Ls), the teller wrote down the amount of the deposit in the saver's bankbook along with any interest that had accrued. In time, computers took over

1

many of these tasks, and the economy started to become more global. In the 1980s and 1990s, banks focused on geographic expansion, entering new markets and building more—and larger—branches. Less than a decade later, the amount of traffic into most retail branches declined sharply. Today, few people visit a brick-and-mortar branch to do their banking. Many banks, especially those with a regional focus, are trying to shutter as many locations as possible, a trend driven largely by the rise of ATM transactions.

The first ATM in the United States appeared sometime in the late 1960s. By 1980, the number of monthly ATM transactions was nearly 100 million. Within 10 years that number grew to almost 500 million transactions per month.[1] This accelerated a strategic change for banking executives. In 20 years, banks went from adding real estate to decreasing real estate—an amazing transformation in a sector that remains the heart of the financial services industry. In the remaining branches, there is also a tighter focus on generating revenue through the sale of specialized products and services that often have higher margins. There are also far fewer tellers than in the past, and it is not uncommon for them to encourage customers to bank online and through mobile channels.

This short trip down memory lane was intentional. Banking is the largest portion of the financial services industry and these rapid changes impacted its employees and clients. In the wake of such significant change to the industry's biggest sector, it's reasonable to believe that the wealth management and advisory businesses will face similar disruption in the very near future. Those opportunities and challenges exist today and will accelerate for advisors.

THE ROOTS OF MODERN INVESTING

The majority of this book is about the future. Our goal is to present a roadmap for increased success in a period of immense change. In order to do so, we believe it is crucial to examine the past. After all, these events have set up where we are today and represent the building blocks

---

[1] Michael Quint. "Citibank Joins Teller Network," *New York Times*, February 16, 1991, www.nytimes.com/1991/02/16/business/company-news-citibank-joins-teller-network.html.

of the future. In the 1950s, most people in the United States shunned investing. Many of them had lived through the Great Depression and wanted no part of the stock market. A number of Americans sub-scribed to the notion that the stock market was for rich people, and this perception had become a reality. Buying and selling securities was costly, in large part because most brokerage firms charged fixed com-missions, which were quite high and typically nonnegotiable. These rates could be 10 percent or more of the transaction amount. In 1952, only 6.5 million Americans, which was about 4.2 percent of the U.S. population, owned stock.[2]

In the 1970s and 1980s, consumers typically looked to brokers for what they deemed to be financial "advice." Madison Avenue helped broker-dealers convey that message to consumers through advertising. One of the most famous commercials of all time was for the brokerage firm, E. F. Hutton. In one commercial, wealthy people were filmed as they lounged around a swimming pool at what appears to be a coun-try club or a fancy hotel. A man turns to a woman and asks about her broker's advice. She answers casually, "Well my broker is E. F. Hutton, and E. F. Hutton says . . ." Everyone around the pool stops talking, purportedly because they want to hear E. F. Hutton's financial advice.

Advertising campaigns like E. F. Hutton's were built on the premise that a brokerage firm could give investors tips on what securities prod-ucts to buy. Since that campaign, the firm has disappeared through a series of acquisitions involving Smith Barney, Morgan Stanley, and Citigroup. (E. F. Hutton's grandson has launched a new, unrelated company under the old name.) But many people remember the slo-gan that made E. F. Hutton famous, "When E. F. Hutton talks, people listen." *Money* magazine describes, on its website, how effective the campaign was during the bull market that began in 1982:

> This was a powerful image during the bull market that
> started in 1982. After the lost decade of the 1970s,
> investors were getting excited about stocks again. The

---

[2] "Stocks Then And Now: 1950s And 1970s," Investopedia, October 1, 2008, www .investopedia.com/articles/stocks/09/stocks-1950s-1970s.asp?layout=orig.

Hutton ad suggested that only through a broker could you gain an investing edge.

In some ways, the suggestion was ironic—coming just ahead of the massive insider trading scandals of the late 1980s, when dozens of Wall Street players, including Ivan Boesky and Michael Milken, were found to have skirted the rules for their own advantage. So much for the broker edge, which in those cases anyway was about illegal stock tips sometimes in exchange for suitcases full of cash.[3]

During that same era, Smith Barney launched an equally memorable ad campaign. Distinguished actor John Houseman voiced the immortal slogan: "Smith Barney. They make money the old-fashioned way: They earn it." It's worth revisiting these advertisements because they capture what the world of financial advice was like in the 1970s and 1980s. And they also reflect how consumers perceived it. These campaigns strongly tied financial advisors to the wealthy classes, and perpetuated the mystique of investment firms. That approach was quite different from what you see today in television commercials for established firms, and in taxi-cab ads for new players like Wealthfront and Betterment.

Firms also operate much differently now. Up until the late 1980s, if you were a broker, you attended a daily research call where stock ideas were discussed. These research calls gave brokers ideas for how to help their clients buy and sell securities. Brokers were allowed to promote only those stocks on which there was research coverage. There's a debate as to why this happened. Some would argue it was to manage risk, as recommended securities should be tracked, but others with a more jaded view argue it was to push the securities with higher commissions or with companies with financial ties to the brokerage firm. The investment business was largely product focused. It was an era when brokers pushed stocks touted by research analysts.

---

[3] "Shhh . . . E.F. Hutton Is Talking Again," *Money*, March 19, 2015, http://time.com/money/3751675/ef-hutton-gateway/.

REGULATORY AND TAX CHANGES SPUR EVOLUTION

In 1975, the Securities and Exchange Commission (SEC) made an important decision that laid the path for the financial world as we know it today. Fixed commissions were abolished. Up until what is known as "May Day," brokerage firms charged commissions based on a schedule published by the New York Stock Exchange. The commission was calculated off a grid based on the number of shares traded. Brokerage firms, therefore, could not compete with each other on price. The new regulations created a situation where commissions could now be negotiated. This decision opened the way for discount brokers, and eventually led to the online trading craze of the 1990s. Fueled by enhanced technology, online trading allowed people to cheaply buy their favorite stocks on their own, without a broker, for the first time.

The next change came in 1978, three years after fixed commissions were abolished. A major change to the tax code opened the door to an entirely new financial services sector. Congress added Section 401, under which Item K allowed companies to offer their employees an additional benefit, now known as the 401(k) retirement savings plan. 401(k)s and similar defined contribution plans helped turn employees from spenders into savers—and investors.

401(k) retirement savings plans took off in the 1980s around the same time that companies began to sunset traditional pensions. The vast majority of defined contribution plans were offered by larger companies as one of the benefits to retain employees and also encourage saving. A key inducement was the employer match, a 401(k) contribution made by the employer at no cost to the employee.

Despite the potential benefits of 401(k) plans, they also presented employers with new challenges. Most companies had no idea how to determine which investments should go into these plans, so they turned to 401(k) record-keeping firms to administer their plans. Most of these firms were units of large mutual fund companies so, not surprisingly, the investment menu consisted of a good range of mutual funds. (The default option was the money market fund, much like today's default option would be a target date fund.) This represented a key building block for the future because the 401(k) business supported the enormous growth of the mutual fund industry.

Meanwhile, wirehouse firms began to more clearly separate business development from managing money. During the 1980s, firms encouraged their account executives to gather new business and increase clients' investments, while professional money managers tended to client portfolios. This shift emerged from the belief that individuals would benefit from the investment professionals' expertise, and that client-facing advisors could better serve customers by focusing more time on their existing clients. Without the burden of managing every client portfolio, advisors could also work on business development.

So marked the beginning of fee-based management and managed accounts. On the heels of the existence of managed accounts came professional gatekeepers who decided which asset managers qualified to be on a securities firm's platform. The good gatekeepers protected clients because the decision to put an asset manager on or off the platform was based on performance. One could argue there were also bad gatekeepers who selected asset managers onto the platform based more on revenue share agreements than what was good for the clients. The debate on good versus bad gatekeepers remains to this day and the managed accounts business has blossomed into a $4 trillion industry.

A SMALL SHIFT TO ADVICE

As we will discuss in depth later in the book, we believe financial planning and coaching will be a key building block of advisor value in the future. When we speak at conferences and industry events, it seems like some people think this is a fundamental change that happened overnight. It's not. The industry has actually been shifting this way for decades. For comparison, consider a musician who has been writing songs and playing in clubs for years. When she finally gets a hit song, she is viewed as an overnight sensation. In reality, however, the musician is being noticed for the first time after years of playing the same kind of music.

Financial planning as a value proposition is nothing new for thousands of advisors. Although in its infancy the idea of *planning* was very different than it is today, it did exist. Back then, the financial planning process focused mostly on asset allocation advice and was often driven by Morningstar-style boxes. The idea of planning gained some attention when the College for Financial Planning opened in 1972. The College has graduated more than 64,000 individuals into the financial planning industry. Can you imagine what it must have been like to graduate in some of those earlier classes? The economic and political factors a planner dealt with in the mid to late 1970s represented uncharted territory. Planners were required to deal with double-digit inflation and a sustained bear market. It was actually a bad time to be in the "advice" business, because the bear market had soured consumers and there were few who wanted to invest. For many consumers, paying close to 18 percent interest on their home mortgages left them with little disposable income. This situation left advisors with fewer potential clients because people were not investing in the market. Consumers with assets were likely keeping their money in certificates of deposit (CDs) or treasuries with longer-term yields above 12 percent.

The 1980s brought a major shift. Faced with making investment selections for their own 401(k) retirement plans, which provided no guidance, people's investment lives started to become more complex. On top of that, the stock market began to recover in 1982 and the tax code was changed in 1986, two changes that made people more interested in the investment potential of the markets. However, the advice business as we think of it today still didn't exist. More money entered the market, but stocks and bonds continued to dominate.

The concepts of holistic advice and account aggregation were not in the lexicon of the day. It was not until the late 1980s that the advice business began to change, and these changes started setting up many of the advice models that exist today. *Fee-only* firms, as they are known today, started popping up around the country. Fee-only firms were built on the idea that the way advisors were paid in the past created conflicts because advisors were paid differently based on the investment products they recommended. Fee-only firms don't collect commissions and don't collect fees from the fund companies for putting their clients in certain securities. The client fees for advice are the only source of revenue for these firms. The argument is since the client is the only one paying the advisory firm, potential conflicts of interest are removed from the relationship. We will drill deeper into this argument later in the book when we discuss how advisors are paid and how consumers should think about fees. Ric Edelman started his firm in 1991, right around the time fee-only advising was going mainstream. When we asked Ric why he decided to start his firm, his answer was simple:

> We went looking for a place where people could get good financial advice and we couldn't find a place like that anywhere. We believed consumers needed people that were focused more on the outcomes they needed in their lives, than the products they needed in their portfolios. The only advice people got was from people focused more on selling them something in their portfolios than bringing better outcomes to their lives.

In the early 1990s, technology use in the industry was exploding and so was the stock market. A trading frenzy enabled by online trading came onto the scene. Charles Schwab was the major disrupter during this time. For the first time, trades were far less expensive than at the major brokerage firms, but the major brokerage firms countered by starting their own online divisions. This intersected with the rise of technology companies nobody had ever heard of—commonly referred to as *dot-coms*. These companies had no real business models, but they became the most talked-about companies in America—and people wanted to feel like they were part of the game. Investing presented them with a way to become directly involved in the action. Regardless of age or wealth tier, people had online accounts to play the market, and they were winning because technology stocks seemed to go in one direction, *up!* Research analysts covering these tech upstarts were measuring them in part by the amount of traffic their websites were getting, which often took precedence over the companies' financials. Later, this time period was famously referred to by Federal Reserve Chairman Alan Greenspan as the period of "irrational exuberance." The dot-com bubble started to burst in 2000, and the stock market slide continued for three years. What is interesting about the market collapse of 2000, and even back to 1987 and 1989, is that consumers seemed to accept that market cycles existed, so unstable periods didn't increase the number of consumers seeking financial advice. We believe this changed with the market turmoil of 2008 and 2009, which we will discuss later in the chapter.

After the technology bubble burst in 2000, many consumers head-ed for the sidelines, but around 2005 a number of online trading tools emerged, offering people a do-it-yourself approach and luring some people back to the markets. During the peak of this trend, you couldn't go to a party without someone talking about their brother, sister, cousin, or unemployed friend who was day trading. Few were day trading full time, but many who were quickly realized they should have kept their day jobs. It's not easy to win against the professionals who dominate market trading. Even more discouraging was the devastating market correction that occurred during the 2008 economic meltdown. Anyone involved in the financial services industry back in 2008—advisor, trad-er, investor—can't help but be scarred from what occurred during the *Great Recession*. People inside the industry and outside of it enjoy debat-ing the merits of quantitative easing or the government bailouts during this time period, but one thing everyone can agree on is how awful late 2008 and 2009 were for those in the financial services industry—espe-cially for all the clients who lost big. It was like a financial Armageddon. It seems nobody was immune. As we mentioned earlier in the chapter, consumers who survived prior market corrections seemed to discon-nect their effects from financial advice or Wall Street anger. Markets go up. Markets go down. That seemed to be the prevailing view of previ-ous corrections. We aren't saying clients weren't frustrated or worried, but given that many of the previous market corrections were at a time when pensions and Social Security were the key retirement vehicles for most Americans, the Great Recession was the first major market correc-tion where everyday investors felt their retirement savings and overall financial health were in jeopardy. The anger, confusion, and growing need for advice triggered an interesting journey for both individual in-vestors and advisors since 2009.

A NEW ADVICE MODEL

In 2008 and 2009, client portfolios were destroyed. When talking to consumers during that time period, many told us they couldn't even open their account statements because they were too anxious to look at them. However, that market cycle, which started in March of 2009, brought about a new approach that correlated with the consumer's perception that investing is easy. The do-it-yourself, day-trading fren-zy that took place just before the financial meltdown was replaced by a hybrid model of simplistic, cost-conscious investments packaged in a digital advice model, the so-called *robo advisor*. The robo-advisor move-ment really began in early 2013 and accelerated throughout that year. As the stock market recovery began to take hold in 2009, the annual returns for the S&P were as follows:

2009: 26 percent

2010: 15 percent

2011: 2 percent

2012: 16 percent

2013: 32 percent

Consumers began to forget about the carnage that occurred in their accounts in 2009. Although consumers were still scared, it certainly started to feel like the markets would go up forever. Despite this, to-day's complex markets mean individual investors need even more reli-able advice than they did in the past.

Too Much Noise

Financial advice is needed now more than ever. Ironically, what makes it more difficult for advisors today is the fact that far more resources are at their disposal. Today's individual investors can obtain financial information from a variety of sources, not just their broker, insurance agent, or financial advisor. Many of these consumers watch CNBC and Fox Business; they read research reports. Financial information (good and bad) is available everywhere. The question for a consumer re-mains the same: Am I receiving objective and disinterested advice?

Jay was in an airport working on this book, and a guy sitting next to him on the plane asked him what he was writing. Jay explained the premise of the book, and it turned out the man was a financial advisor. The guy laughed and said, "I knew consumers had too much free advice at their disposal when I got a call from my 78-year-old mother. She was calling to ask me why we weren't shorting a stock in her account because she heard it discussed on Jim Cramer's *Mad Money* television program." It really is an ironic twist. Consumers have gone from getting little or no financial data to suffering from information overload but, with this change, the consumer is no better off. Many people would argue that investors should put that information to good use and do more research before making investment decisions, but when you spend time with the people, you quickly realize few have the time or the interest to sift through the information available to them. With apologies to Jim Cramer and E. F. Hutton, investment advice today should encompass much more than hot stock tips.

Changes in Investment Products

Just as the advice model has changed for consumers over the past five decades, so have the investment products and solutions in their portfolios. In the 1950s and 1960s, most portfolios consisted of stocks and bonds. That was it. There were no mutual funds or exchange-traded funds (ETFs) or any of the other, more sophisticated investment products that exist today. If you were one of the 4.6 percent of Americans during that time period with investments in the market, you probably owned blue-chip stocks like IBM and corporate bonds like those offered by General Electric. In the 1970s, investors graduated into partnerships; commonly oil and gas limited partnerships driven by the oil boom. In the 1980s, some investors began to move toward fee-based brokerage accounts, but it wasn't a large movement.

The setup for many of today's investment vehicle trends occurred in the 1990s with mutual fund superstars like Peter Lynch of Magellan. Lynch claimed that during his time at the firm, one out of every 100 Americans with investable assets put them in the Magellan mutual fund.

Mutual funds were touted as a way for small investors to diversify their nest egg. Initially, most mutual funds were actively managed by a fund manager who selected which stocks to include. Later, mutual funds tied to market indexes like the S&P 500 became popular.

The separately managed account (SMA) was also on the rise in the 1990s. Separately managed accounts were touted as highly personalized accounts, managed to meet the specific needs of a single investor. For all the talk around these new products, SMAs were not customized as many consumers believed. Instead they were just packaged strategies. The manager actively traded stocks with the goal of using a particular strategy to outpace the overall market.

In 1991, the first consumer ETF was launched, but it took some time for these new products to gain momentum. Today, many financial advisors' strategies are built around ETFs, and they are the building blocks of many robo-advisor or digital portfolios. The rapid growth of ETF utilization has surprised many, including us. Chip Roame, managing partner of Tiburon Strategic Advisors, is similarly amazed:

> I wrote off ETFs initially because I didn't think they were
> attractive in the way they were being sold. Originally
> the differentiation salespeople discussed was that, unlike
> mutual funds, ETFs could be traded and valued throughout
> the day. I remember thinking, "Who cares?" What I and
> so many others missed was the appeal investors saw in
> passive indexing at much lower product costs.

The ETF marketplace now represents $4.1 trillion in assets or 15 percent of the overall mutual fund universe. ETFs have many advantages for end investors. Even the SEC commissioner has taken notice of the benefits of the vehicles for investors. ETFs, according to SEC Commissioner Kara M. Stein in a speech at Harvard Law School on November 9, 2015, have been in some ways a "positive, competitive innovation in the markets. They have opened up an array of investment options for investors and are often more tax efficient." Her continued comments on ETF behavior could be signaling an interesting focus as the SEC and other regulatory agencies deal with their growing utilization in digital portfolios. According to Stein, ETFs behave very differently than mutual funds—*very* differently.

On August 24, 2015, many stocks opened extremely and unexpectedly low. Certain stocks dropped almost 50 percent and then quickly recovered for no apparent reason. Trading was halted 1,200 times that day. But that rocky day demonstrated that ETFs may act quite unusually in stressed market conditions. ETFs should trade relatively closely to the overall fair value of the underlying stocks in the ETF. Throughout the day there were a number of times where this did not occur, where wide variances existed between certain ETFs' traded values and the value of the underlying securities. This has an impact on the liquidity of the ETF. Liquidity and interday valuations/trading, on paper, are supposed to be key benefits of ETF vehicles.

Stein expressed concern for everyday investors who submitted stop loss orders on August 24. There were numerous reports of investors who found that their shares were sold at a price well below their stop loss orders, which defeated the purpose of the stop loss orders, which is to cut an investor's losses when a security is dropping in price. In the end, ETFs, in many advisors' and investors' eyes, have brought some key benefits to the end investor. The key benefit being the ability to access diversified investments at a much lower cost. Regardless of these recent comments from the SEC, it is clear that ETFs are not only here to stay, but also a continued growth segment of the investment product universe.

Changing Technology

As an industry, we tend to look at today's technology as if it's extremely disruptive. Although this is true, the technology revolution didn't just arrive; it's been incrementally impacting the business for over eight decades. As we were finalizing this chapter, someone correctly pointed out that we didn't go far enough back in talking about technology's impact. The technology impact on the securities industry goes all the way back to the universal ownership of the automobile. Up until the 1940s, most people with financial assets lived in cities. The ownership of the automobile caused geographic dispersion. Suddenly firms wishing to do business with the wealthy opened branches outside the cities. Charlie Merrill was the leader, with his campaign: "Bring Wall Street to Main Street." Technology was so expensive, only the largest firms could afford it and do business with it. The biggest firms on Wall Street had the advantage because they were the only ones with certain information.

A look back at personal finance articles through the decades has to make you laugh given where we are today as advisors and investors. In a December 1983 article in *Changing Times* magazine, the predecessor of *Kiplinger*, the author took note of the computer blitz:

> As in so many other fields, the computers have taken over
> in financial planning. The odds are that the information you
> give the planner will be fed into a computer and massaged
> into impressive arrays of figures. The more sophisticated
> programs can perform marvels such as calculating taxes in
> various ways to find the lowest-cost method.[4]

At a time when Elon Musk was warning the United Nations to ban work on artificial intelligence robots because of his concern they might take over the planet, tax-calculating computer software hardly seems groundbreaking.

As the United States and other countries struggle to keep ahead of hackers and terrorists, what is often overlooked is the regulatory change necessary to deal with the advancing technology landscape. These regulatory changes are particularly challenging in the financial services industry. Although this seems like a small issue, it's relevant to firms trying to build their value proposition for small accounts using digital technologies. Commissioner Stein observed that the SEC is now thinking about what it means to regulate a robo advisor, a concept that did not exist when most of the laws governing investment advisors were drafted. Stein stated:

> What does a fiduciary duty even look like or mean
> for a robo advisor? The idea of a robotic entity that
> automatically generates investment advice certainly
> bumps up against what we would traditionally think of as
> a fiduciary. As this innovation gains more market share (as
> it seems poised to do), we should be asking whether these
> new robo advisors can be neatly placed within our existing
> laws. Or, do we need certain tweaks and revisions? Do
> investors using robo advisors appreciate that, for all their
> benefits, robo advisors will not be on the phone providing
> counsel if there is a market crash?[5]

Keep in mind that the Investment Advisers Act became effective in 1940.

---

[4] "Financial Planners—How to Find the Right One," *Changing Times* (December 1983), p. 30.

[5] Commissioner Kara M. Stein, "Surfing the Wave: Technology, Innovation, and Competition–Remarks at Harvard Law School's Fidelity Guest Lecture Series," November 9, 2015, www.sec.gov/news/speech/stein-2015-remarks-harvard-law-school.html.

We believe that robo technology that offers investors a 100 percent do-it-yourself approach will present challenges to most consumers. We believe it's analogous to the pursuit of driverless cars. In 1989, the movie *Back to the Future 2* predicted we would have flying cars by 2015. This seems just as unbelievable and futuristic today as it did then. However, it seems certain we will have driverless cars someday, likely before flying cars are possible. Although prototypes are in the works, we still don't have driverless cars, let alone flying automobiles. Will we get there one day as a society? It's likely. However, the pursuit of the goal has been much more expensive and much more difficult than those inventing them believed it would be.

This isn't some off-the-wall tangent. In researching the pursuit of driverless cars, we found the pursuit parallels the emergence of do-it-yourself financial advice technologies. It isn't the mechanics of driver-less cars that is impeding their adoption. The technology is currently failing when things don't go as planned: a human driver doesn't follow the rules at a stop sign, or there's rapid lane change by a driver texting and drinking coffee while driving. These anomalies require quick as-sessment and reaction that computers have yet to figure out. Sound familiar? Like driverless cars, the markets work most of the time, un-der typical conditions. It's when the markets are volatile that consum-ers need advice. Assessing the do-it-yourself capabilities during the majority of the time or in periods of normalcy may lead investors to very different conclusions on the need for human financial advice. When the market swings like a crazy driver switching lanes, the true role of professional advice needs to be assessed.

The financial services industry has come a long way over the past five decades. It continues to move from being product centered to be-ing advice centered, and technology and regulations continue to push advisors to do things differently, hopefully for the better.

Our journey through the past in this chapter was designed to set up the realities of where we are going in the industry. We interviewed a wide variety of industry leaders, practitioners, and consultants. One of the questions we asked everyone was, "How disruptive do you see the current forces being on the future of the financial services industry?" The answers were across the board, with some people saying it's a con-sumer revolution, not an evolution, and others believing that every

10 years something disrupts the industry, but good advisors can help their clients weather the storm. We will sort through these differing opinions in the coming chapters. In the end, clients need advice and we as an industry are here to deliver it.

 ## THE CONSUMER PERSPECTIVE

Pam Krueger believes consumers should have realized that up until the mid-1980s, people invested for only two reasons: (1) they were well off and wanted to continue building their wealth, or (2) they wanted to play in the market. The average American didn't feel as compelled to invest because Social Security and a company pension was enough to fund retirement; investments weren't necessary. Average investors still kept their money in bank accounts and CDs. They trusted their employers and the government, and they had secure futures. Most Americans didn't have to make investment choices, because their pension plans did the investing for them. As the 401(k) came online, it democratized the investment process. The financial services industry saw this as a positive change because it put the investor in charge. On balance, it has been a good thing. However, as people are forced to make more decisions on their own, it has caused consumers to become frightened. This fear has led to inertia, which causes investors to do nothing. To give themselves the opportunity to achieve their financial goals, it is imperative that investors be proactive.

When consumers were less dependent upon investing to fund their retirement and other long-term goals, dabbling in the stock market was viewed as a hobby. If they invested in a company that lost money or went bankrupt, it was upsetting, but not dream crushing. But today's investors are in an entirely different situation. On the one hand, they are far less likely to have pensions and, with interest rates near zero, today's consumers must become active investors if they hope to retire and achieve other life goals. On the other hand, a negative investment outcome could be devastating.

Digitizing

The financial industry is really proud of itself for coming up with all kinds of great tools. However, these tools might give the consumer vertigo. In some cases, these tools have driven assets to places like Schwab and Vanguard, brands that have successfully communicated the value of automated advice. The digital tools that the industry is so proud of have only caused bigger problems for consumers. For those who are already apprehensive about making investment choices—and suffering the consequences—alone, digital tools can seem even more daunting and lonely.

The Trust Gap

A trust gap remains where even consumers that do seek advice are hesitant to follow it. See Figure 1.1. In 2013, one in four consumers who paid for advice implemented 100 percent of the advice. The number one reason cited for not following that advice was lack of trust. Given the scandals of the 1980s and 1990s along with this heightened need for the returns on investments, it's easy to see why a trust gap exists between the investing public and the industry.

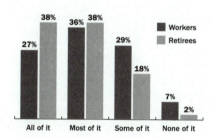

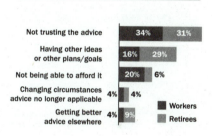

Figure 1.1 The Trust Gap

KEY TAKEAWAYS

- Although the pace of change is picking up in the financial services industry, reacting to changes has always been the hallmark of successful advisors. Consumers feel either empowered or frightened and overwhelmed into inertia. By failing to do anything with their money, it loses value and fails to keep pace with inflation. To overcome inertia, consumers want someone to drive the car for them.
- The push and pull between technology and regulations are going to be a major driver of future industry change.

- While the industry moves from product centered to advice centered, the investment products in client portfolios have changed and will continue to do so.

- The pressure has mounted on clients to achieve positive investment outcomes to reach their goals. It is unlikely they will have a pension to plug the gap between their Social Security income and what it will take to live a comfortable retirement.

- The trust gap that exists between the industry and the investor will continue to be a problem that advisors need to overcome.

CHAPTER **2**

The Evolution
of Complexity

*Any intelligent fool can make things bigger, more
complex . . . it takes a touch of genius—and a lot of
courage—to move in the opposite direction.*

—Albert Einstein

We believe the value of advice is driven by an advisor's ability
to simplify the complex for the end consumer. Thus, the demand for advice will be directly correlated to the complexity
experienced by the end consumer. So the important question is: Is
the end consumer's life more complex or less complex than it was
10 years ago?

Imagine a couple browsing in a high-end store that sells everything they could possibly need for their kitchen. A young man working on the showroom floor offers them a cappuccino to enjoy while
they shop. The couple happily takes him up on his offer and the sales-
man heads over to a $3,000 espresso machine in one of the model
areas. After 10 minutes of trying, he gives up because the machine is
too complicated to operate. Determined to deliver the cappuccinos, the
man finally resorts to using a much less expensive machine to make
the drinks. The end result is likely just as good as what the high-end
machine would have delivered.

In recent years, financial-advice consumers have felt a similar pain, as advisors sometimes make things more complicated than necessary.

TALKING ABOUT MY GENERATION

For young people, there is nothing worse than hearing a parent tell a story that begins with, "When I was a child . . ." Inevitably, stories like this end with parents telling their children how much more difficult their lives were by comparison. The story is usually punctuated by an eye roll from the child.

Jane Buckingham is the founder and president of Trendera, a consumer insights group, and the author of *The Modern Girl's Guide to Life*. She is considered to be an expert on marketing to different generations. Buckingham made this point in a magazine article:

> Every generation thinks they've had it harder than the previous one. It's really comparing apples and oranges. I understand why we do it—it's our only frame of reference. The best way to try to understand what a generation is going through is to try not to think about it from your own perspective, and instead, talk to the people of that generation. For example, I tell my kids that social media today makes life harder on them because your popularity is summed up by a number of likes or followers, or you always know there is another party happening or that your best friends are hanging out without you. Yet it's all they have really ever known. So it's not worse; it's their own reality. They have to grow up knowing how to handle it, which is different from how I had to deal with things.[1]

While this is true in some respects, when it comes to financing college, younger generations do face more complications. There's an old joke that goes something like this: "Thank you, student loans, for helping me get through college. I can never repay you." For many Millennials and Generation Xers, student loans are nothing to joke about.

According to a Harris Poll survey conducted on behalf of the American Institute of CPAs (AICPA), more than one-third of college students

---

[1] *Me&V Magazine*, January 2016, 48–49.

who enrolled in the 2015 fall semester expect to live at home because of student loan debt. On average, college students with loans anticipated paying off their loans in nine years after graduation. Eighteen percent thought it would take more than 10 years.[2]

The AICPA's press release reported this startling finding on November 12, 2015:

> While a college education is often a stepping stone to financial security, the high cost of individual student loans may be forcing many students to postpone major decisions such as marriage, having children, purchasing a home, or saving for retirement. Many students also said their loans mean they would likely be living with their parents after graduation and might have to take a job outside their field of study (37 percent each).[3]

The survey reported that:

- Fifty-nine percent of borrowing college students believed they would repay their loans in full within 10 years.
- Seventy-nine percent did not know what the exact total amount of their loans would be upon graduation.
  - Forty-three percent had a general idea of the amount they had borrowed.
  - Thirty-six percent had either no idea or only a vague estimate of their total loan amount.
- Twenty-two percent knew exactly what their loan total would be upon graduation.

THE NOT-SO-SIMPLE LIFE

In many respects, consumers' lives are much more complicated today than they once were. In the *good old days*, employees worked for the same company for years—often for their entire careers. Most

---

[2] Tim Grant, "Study: One-Third of College Grads Plan to Move Back Home," *The Palm Beach Post*, December 6, 2015, D-2.

[3] "One-Third of College Students Say They'll Live at Home Post-Graduation Due to Loan Debt," November 12, 2015, www.aicpa.org/press/pressreleases/2015/pages/college-students-live-home-due-to-loan-debt.aspx.

had defined benefit plans that supplied pension payments once they reached a specified age in retirement. Employer-sponsored medical insurance was often covered in full as a benefit, even for retirees. Today, many companies no longer offer health-care benefits to retirees, who must consider that as they plan for retirement and old age.

In the 1970s, college tuition at some state schools was $500 a term or less. Today, parents sometimes have to choose between putting away money for retirement and paying their child's tuition. Despite steep tuition increases, more people are pursuing graduate degrees, which can put additional financial stress on the parents of adult children.

A survey from Pew Research posted online on January 30, 2013, illustrated how complicated life can be for members of the so-called *sandwich generation*. The term refers to middle-aged adults who are sandwiched between caring for aging parents and raising children.[4] Nearly half of adults in their 40s and 50s have a parent who is age 65 or older and are either raising a young child or providing support to a grown child who is age 18 or older.

Two-thirds of Americans over age 65 are expected to need some type of long-term care at some point in their lives. Long-term care policies have become increasingly expensive. Even consumers who bought policies at a young age have been subjected to huge rate hikes because long-term care insurers found themselves paying out much more in claims than they anticipated. As a result, a number of long-term care insurers have stopped offering these policies.

Caring for an elderly parent or grandparent has become far more difficult and expensive for families. According to Genworth's 2015 study, the median charge for a private room in a nursing home is $91,250 per year. A semiprivate room isn't much cheaper. The median annual cost is $80,300. The cost of nursing home care has risen far more rapidly than inflation.

The statistics are frightening. Roughly half of adults age 40 to 59 have provided support to at least one grown child during the past year. In 27 percent of the cases, adults were providing the child's primary

---

[4] Kim Parker, "The Sandwich Generation: Rising Financial Burdens for Middle-Aged Americans," January 30, 2013, www.pewsocialtrends.org/2013/01/30/the-sandwich-generation/.

support. On the other side of the coin, about one in five middle-aged adults have provided financial support in the past year to a parent who is age 65 or older. Among all adults, 75 percent said they owe a duty to provide financial assistance to an elderly parent who is in need. Roughly one in seven middle-aged adults provides financial support to both a parent and child.

The Tech Dimension

A survey from Bankrate.com revealed that 46 percent of Americans reported that they or somebody they knew had been a victim of identity fraud. In a different era, it was rare to hear of anyone's identity being stolen.

Aside from identity theft, many consumers live in fear that their computers will be hacked and their most personal information will be stolen. Major financial services firms have been the targets of cyber attacks and even government websites have been hacked. This is just a small example of how advising clients today and into the future will get more complex. Should advisors be advising clients about buying identify theft protection? If so, should it be defensive or offensive? The defensive approach may be handled by adding identify theft repair riders to their home insurance policy. The offensive approach may include purchasing identify theft monitoring through their bank or through a stand-alone technology company like LifeLock. From the consumer's perspective, this is an added expense to the household budget that didn't exist even five years ago.

Consumers also now have information and entertainment at their fingertips with a cost that is astounding when compared to what consumers once paid for having roofs over their heads. Today, monthly cell phone plans cost more than many consumers paid for their mortgages in the 1970s. It used to be that consumers paid for each minute spent on a cell phone. The charge was similar to paying a broker's commission for each transaction. Cell phone carriers today keep reinventing how they get paid. The minutes are the commodity. Data is where the money is made. Financial advisors may need to take note of this simple example. As the item provided becomes commoditized, the cell phone companies changed their model and invented new services clients needed. They charge premiums for these new services as the fees from the traditional services decline.

THE CHALLENGES OF THE FAMILY ADVISOR

The complexity of issues facing the sandwich generation, which also represents the group that holds a large percentage of current and future investable assets, creates challenges for firms serving their financial planning needs. It also offers a tremendous opportunity for them. Imagine the dilemma firms face when working with a client forced to make a decision about a parent's health-care costs. A strong bond between advisor and client can be engendered if an advisor is able to assist a client who is forced to make a heartbreaking decision about a parent's elder care, the family's health-care options, or how to help an adult child find a job and move out of the basement. These are choices that can affect the financial well-being of every member of the household. This is real value, especially for the client who was looking forward to an empty nest and a pool table in the basement.

In his book, *The Business of Life*, Michael F. Kay discussed how complicated clients' lives have become:

> For financial planners in particular, the needs of our clients are becoming exponentially more complex. The numbers are easy to acquire but they just don't tell the whole story. In addition to the numbers, I've learned, we need to understand behaviors, habits and what motivates people (including ourselves) to live a fuller and richer life. Many planners have difficulty asking the tough questions, feeling it is too invasive or uncomfortable for them and for their clients. For this reason, they may not know their clients well enough to be able to help them make the decisions that are most closely aligned with their values and dreams.[5]

According to Kay, traditional financial planning utilizes a quantitative approach to understanding a client through numbers. A life planning approach marries the numbers with a deep and considered knowledge and understanding of the clients' goals, needs, aspirations, and expectations.[6]

---

[5] Michael F. Kay, *The Business of Life* (Sunnyvale, CA: Advisor Press, 2010), 3.
[6] Ibid, 11.

As life increases in complexity, it becomes even more important for consumers to have financial plans. At the start of the financial planning process, clients articulate and examine their goals. The plan should be holistic, which means it looks at all of the interrelated parts such as income, expenses, investments, debt, retirement planning, risk management, and estate planning. A solid financial plan includes a series of solid and specific recommendations that are designed to help consumers reach their goals.

It is extremely difficult for consumers to reach their goals when they are being pulled in a number of directions. Dual income households continue to rise as does the length of the average work day. The same hardworking people may be thrust into caregiving roles for not only their children, but also their parents. Most clients today feel like Figure 2.1.

We posed a simple question to Jim Pratt-Heaney, cofounder of LLBH Private Wealth: "Is life more complex or less complex than it was 10 years ago for your clients?" He didn't hesitate: "It's much tougher on our clients, and they absolutely need us more." Jim said residence issues related to taxes have become a much bigger issue for his clients.

Figure 2.1 The Consumer's Complexity

"We used to see clients who would not let the tax tail wag the dog. Clients weren't going to move to Florida and live somewhere just for tax reasons. However, that seems to be changing, and it causes a real strain on families." He also talked about the importance of family meetings. "We have always believed family meetings are important in order to get multiple generations on the same page, but the need to have these meetings has increased. The kids and grandkids aren't finding jobs. The grandparents are upset about it. It just causes a lot of anxiety," he said.

Pratt-Heaney's firm was forced to hire an international development person because of the way money moves around, as well as the need for tax sheltering. Pratt-Heaney told us that the complexity of estate planning is "insane" compared to five years ago.

Financial advisors can help clients with questions that used to be relatively simply to answer. In another era, when faced with the decision of whether to buy a home or rent, it was a no-brainer for financial advisors. In almost every instance, advisors recommended that clients buy a home instead of renting. Today, the decision is far from clear-cut. Clients are unlikely to stay rooted to the same job for years to come. A financial advisor must look at taxes, maintenance, the cost of rental properties, insurance, and other expenses tied to home ownership. Financial advisors help their clients decide if it is better to buy a home and build equity or to rent and invest the savings and down payment.

It is not just younger clients who must choose between buying and renting. Jodi Helmer wrote an article for *MarketWatch* that analyzed whether consumers should buy or rent in retirement. Although retirees are accustomed to the idea of homeownership, there are real advantages to renting. According to the article, retirees and preretirees considering downsizing often struggle with the decision of whether to rent or buy. The upside to renting is that a retiree can try out living in a smaller home or one-story living. Retirees can see if they like the area before making the huge commitment of buying a house. As a renter and not a homeowner, retirees avoid a down payment, maintenance and repair costs, property taxes, and condo association fees.[7]

Financial advisors can help clients, young or old, address these issues objectively and unemotionally using tools such as the Beracha,

---

[7] Jodi Helmer, "Should You Rent or Buy in Retirement?" *MarketWatch*, December 30, 2015, www.marketwatch.com/story/should-you-rent-or-buy-in-retirement-2015-12-30.

Hardin & Johnson Buy vs. Rent Index. The index is designed to signal whether current market conditions favor buying or renting a home in terms of wealth creation. The index looks at specific markets in relation to historical market conditions, as well as alternative investment opportunities. Whereas buying a home was once a fundamental element of the American Dream, it is not necessarily the right choice for every client. As we will see in Chapter 6, buying a first home is one of the important life transitions that prompt consumers to engage advisors.

Advisors' Complicated Lives

The world is noisy, even for advisors. Financial advisors are bombarded 24/7 with information overload. The realities of trying to not only serve clients but also run a growing business can be overwhelming. Most advisors feel like Figure 2.2. The scrutiny of regulators, as well as the speed at which new tools are being implemented due to client

Figure 2.2 The Advisors' Complexity

demand, has advisors running fast. Social media is only one small example. Financial advisors who market and communicate using social media must be ever vigilant. They need to be cognizant of comments and communications made on Facebook, LinkedIn, Twitter, blogs, and other forms of social media.

A financial advisor's reputation can be damaged with just a few keystrokes. Decades ago, unhappy clients would make disparaging comments about an advisor to friends, relatives, and business associates. Today, however, they can tell the world about their negative experiences with an advisor instantaneously in online reviews.

We were lucky enough to have a number of industry leaders sit down with us to discuss content for the book. One of the questions we asked a number of them in our discussions was this: "What's one thing you think the industry or advisors are missing about the future value equation?" Before answering that question, it is helpful to look at the terminology that our industry uses without considering that it is a foreign language to consumers.

Registered investment advisors (RIAs) are firms that are regulated by the SEC or state securities regulators. Generally, RIAs are registered with the SEC if they have assets under management (AUM) of $100 million or more. The advice at an RIA is provided by an investment advisor representative (IAR). RIAs and IARs are held to a fiduciary standard, which means they must act in the best interest of their clients. Though this seems like basic information, we've run into financial planners who don't realize their firm is the RIA and they are the IAR.

Over the last few years, we have seen clients and advisors make the break from wirehouses, which are large brokerage firms, to what we call the independent space or channel. These advisors leave their jobs as registered representatives for broker-dealers to open their own RIAs. In most cases, they are trying to escape the sales culture of the wirehouse. Not all RIAs are independent, however. There's a blurring of the channels. Some corporate RIAs are tied to a hybrid model with a broker-dealer relationship. Regardless, the RIA landscape is making the advisor market more competitive.

Shirl Penney, CEO of Dynasty Financial Partners, believes advisors don't recognize the growing amount of competition in the independent space, and also the sophistication of that competition. Penney said:

> Many advisors in the RIA fee-only space were early adopters
> of this new fiduciary model when they started and grew
> their firms. It was easy for them to differentiate themselves as
> fiduciaries when they were taking on the brokers and banks.
> However, that's changing as the breakaway movement picks
> up speed. RIAs are going to compete a lot more with each
> other and this is going to make differentiation even harder.

Dynasty alone helped launch three RIAs with assets under management that exceeded $1 billion in 2015. Stats from InvestmentNews echo Penney's comments. 2015 was a record year for breakaway assets leaving the banks and wirehouses with a declining amount of those assets switching from one wirehouse to another.

Penney's point is a good one. There's also one more key consideration relevant to Penney's comments. The increased volume of the breakaway movement is going to complicate the business models of many advisors. It will also challenge the culture of many firms. There are a lot of reasons why some of the legacy business models are broken. These models may result in conflicted advice, fee structures that are unfair to the end consumer, and compensation grids that blur the actual amount of fees paid to the advisor.

We could go on and on about the conflicts of interest, but there is one thing about the wirehouse culture that cannot be ignored—the sales culture. You survive in a wirehouse for one reason, and that's because you can sell. The entire model is built so brokers minimize their time doing back office functions, and they maximize the time they spend with clients. This laser focus on bringing in new clients, when combined with a fiduciary model, creates a very hard combination to beat. This is why many breakaway firms have been so successful.

Many firms today are client centered, not business centered. We admire the outstanding service these firms provide to their current clients. However, they focus little on the business itself and the development of it. Although this model has worked well in the past, it won't work in the future for the firms who really want to grow. The complexity of competing with the breakaway RIAs will require an entirely new outlook on the business.

Chip Roame echoed these sentiments. Roame said he believes the complexity of the future is going to cause a major bifurcation between the firms that grow and the firms that don't. He believes this bifurcation is going to be caused by the need to invest significant dollars in marketing, and differentiation is already starting to play out in the numbers. "Look at the largest RIAs in the country, Edelman and Fisher as an example, and their growth is enormous. They have a major advantage against the competition because their size gives them the opportunity to invest in a brand," Roame said. Edelman and Fisher are examples of firms with personal brands, scalable across multiple media platforms. They are a rarity as there are approximately 1,000 RIAs today with more than $1 billion in assets managed and few are growing at their rates.

Roame's comments are particularly interesting if you step back and play them out over the entire industry. They illustrate that, if the largest firms are creating most of the additional assets under management, then a majority of the firms in the marketplace are not growing. In fact, their lack of growth is hidden by the performance of the top performers. According to the 2015 Cerulli RIA Marketplace Report, the top 7 percent of advisors by size manage 69 percent of the dually registered and RIA assets. This has very real ramifications on this cycle of complexity for the clients, because firms that cannot grow lack the ability to invest in growing talent or improving the client experience. The cycle of complexity for firms is only going to continue.

NEEDS AND WANTS

We are all consumers. We buy goods: computers, phones, and laundry detergent. We buy services: dry-cleaning, car washes, and airline tickets. How do we determine what to buy? Generally, consumers are stimulated to buy based on either a perceived need or a perceived want. We need water. We want a pair of Gucci shoes. Absent a need or a want, consumers don't purchase.

The next step in making a buying choice is the definition and assessment of value relative to price. This isn't an economics book, so we'll continue on down the path of walking the line between insight and oversimplification for the sake of brevity. If consumers see value, they are willing to pay more. If they can't tell the difference in value, they choose on the basis of price. However, in a world where people pay $5 for a cup of coffee, it's easy to see how value selling still exists. This is very easy to understand when walking through the example of buying a product. However, when consumers buy services, a distinction exists in how a consumer assesses the transaction. That distinction is extremely important for advisors.

When purchasing services, consumers still have a need and want process. However, the assessment of "need" is arguably more difficult for complex transactions, like financial services. How do consumers assess whether they need advice? And if they need it, what kind do they need?

Most of them don't know how. Michael Kitces, an industry-leading consultant, writer, and speaker, talked to us about this exact problem. "As an industry, we continue to talk about financial planning being at the center of what we do for clients. What does that mean? The consumer doesn't understand what planning is because every advisor delivers a different product under that term," he said. Today, advisors spend an immense amount of time engaged in the prospecting process. Much of advisors' time is spent just getting prospective clients to determine if they need advice, or giving them free advice to hook the purchase of future advice.

For the consumer, there's also a decision of relative need versus relative complexity, which drives the value equation for an advisory service. Consumers may get to a point ultimately where they know they need to do something, but then have no idea how to determine value. Decisions are based on price when a consumer thinks the value between two objects is exactly the same. However, consumers make choices without even being able to tell if value exists because they don't understand how to assess it. In this situation, consumers don't decide on price; they don't make a decision at all.

This is how our industry has spawned a subset of people who are willing to take a self-service approach to investing or, even worse, people do nothing at all and hope things work out. As an industry, we have lacked the ability to describe how advisors add value (outside of money management), and, in many cases, we have lacked the ability to help consumers understand the risks of going it alone.

This is going to seem like we are talking out of both sides of our mouth: One of our recurring points throughout this book is that the consumer needs greater simplicity to understand what advisors do and the benefits they provide. It is not because consumers aren't smart enough to understand what advisors do. The problem is that we have complicated the industry with jargon, and it isn't worth a consumer's time to try to navigate the complexity. Consumers who have invested for long periods of time don't want to be educated; they just want it to be done for them. When you spend time with Bill Schiffman, president and cofounder of Schiffman Grow & Company, it's hard not to laugh. He has an interesting way of describing what he does for his clients: "I cut their financial lawns." What? Schiffman goes further to explain the comment which on the surface seems very odd:

> I can cut my own grass. I choose not to because I feel like my time is better spent doing other things. I would stack my clients' intelligence against anyone else's in the business. All of my clients could ultimately manage their own money or do their own taxes. They choose not to. They maximize the value of their time by allowing me to do these things for them.

Financial publications and educational websites helped investors become more comfortable with investing. They touted strategies like dollar-cost averaging and dividend reinvestment as surefire ways to invest successfully over the long haul. They convinced many investors that, in the long run, staying the course would lead to a successful outcome.

The Formula Fallacy

Financial books and magazines have taught investors to use calculation shortcuts like the Rule of 72. If an investor's rate of return was 8 percent, the person's nest egg would double in nine years, since 72 divided by 8 equals 9. And if an investor managed to achieve a rate of return of 12 percent, his or her nest egg would double in six years. By dividing the magic number of 72 by 12, this simple math formula projected that the investor's principal would double in six years. There was just one tiny little problem for the investor. Sometimes, they didn't average 8 percent or 12 percent in returns. In fact, sometimes their nest eggs dropped by 50 percent.

Financial educators convinced some investors that asset allocation is easy. They would espouse asset allocation formulas, which stated that investors should subtract their age from the number 100 to determine how much of their portfolios to keep in stock. Using this formula, 40-year-olds should have 60 percent of their portfolios in stock since 100 minus 40 equals 60. Sixty-year-olds should have 40 percent of their portfolios in the stock market, because 100 minus 60 is 40.

However, these financial rules of thumb espoused by the media are no substitute for sophisticated financial planning and can do more harm than good. Even when investors understand they should have 60 percent of their portfolios in the stock market, they usually aren't aware of how to diversify that portion of their nest eggs. As the SEC's Office of Investor Education and Advocacy pointed out in *Investor Bulletin: Behavioral Patterns of U.S. Investors,* "Inadequate diversification occurs when an investor's portfolio is too concentrated in a particular type of investment. Inadequate diversification increases the risk exposure of an investor's portfolio."[8]

The *Investor Bulletin* also warned about other investing behaviors that can undermine performance such as naïve diversification. According to the publication:

> Naïve diversification occurs when an investor, given
> a number of investment options, chooses to invest
> equally in all of these options. While this strategy may
> not necessarily result in diminished performance, it
> may increase the risk exposure of an investor's portfolio
> depending upon the risk level of each investment option.[9]

Another variation of this risk is the risk of picking previous winners, assuming past performance is indicative of future returns. We see this is as a common issue with 401(k) asset selections. When new employees sign up for allocations, it's difficult for them to look at the choices, see the track records of past performance, and not assume the past winners will be future winners. As we know, some may be and some may not be.

---

[8] *Investor Bulletin: Behavioral Patterns of U.S. Investors,* June 16, 2014, www.sec.gov/oiea/investor-alerts-bulletins/ib_behavioralpatterns.html.
[9] Ibid.

Many investors also mistakenly believe their portfolios are diversified because they have invested in several mutual funds or ETFs. They may not be aware that these mutual funds and ETFs they've invested in have similar investment objectives and hold many of the same securities. In some cases, investors believe the simple solution is to invest in target-date funds based on their expected year of retirement. Unfortunately, the choice of a target-date fund ignores the fact that the investor has other goals aside from retirement. Those goals, such as funding a child's education or taking a dream vacation, are separate and distinct from retirement and often come round much sooner. Consumers also tend to believe all target-date funds are created equal. When you review performance of them for the same date, given the different asset class weightings throughout, it's no different than any other investment vehicle that would have different performance outcomes regardless of the target date being the same.

THE SEARCH FOR SIMPLICITY

It's easy to see why the consumer would want simplicity from the industry. There's a delicate balance for advisors, as being too complex, as we discussed earlier, is a challenge. However, oversimplifying portfolio design aspects of the advice business through the past two decades has also made it seem as if asset allocation and investment decisions are something you can pick and choose from (check out some of the great names of the portfolios as well):

- Bill Schultheis's Coffeehouse Portfolio
- Allan Roth's Second Grader Portfolio
- David Swenson's Ivy League Portfolio
- William Bernstein's No Brainer Portfolio

For the most part, these "recommended strategies" consisted of ETF portfolios. As we will discuss later, the value an advisor drives is much more than just initial portfolio design. However, if consumers think simply picking a portfolio solution from a list (and there are hundreds out there) will get them to their desired outcomes, why would they think they need financial advice?

The Purpose Should Transcend the Complexity

A good friend of ours, Zachary Karabell, author of *The Leading Indicators* and many other successful books on the financial services industry, talks often about how the financial industry has so quickly forgotten its roots: "The industry itself is called the financial *services* industry. As advisors and other members of the industry, we must not forget the role we play. This role must be evident in how we operate our firms." He said: "It is also important that we be seen as playing a valuable role in our clients' eyes. They must see that there's an important reason for us to do what we do every day of the week."

Though life seems as if it was much simpler decades ago, the American Dream can still be attained. Young people will need a wider skill set in order to achieve it. They won't achieve their goals by working at the same job for the next 30 years.

Millennial Investors

Not many people realize that Millennials, the generation born after 1980, were impacted more than anyone by the market meltdown in 2008. They watched their parents lose jobs and savings. The meltdown truly impacted their views on investing, Wall Street, and corporate America. Some of them are afraid of the market and fearful of investing. Generally, Millennials are afraid that if they invest $5, they'll have $3 down the road. This fear discourages them from investing at all. A recent study from McAdam, an independent financial planning firm, found that Millennials tend to be more wary of financial advisors than older investors.[10]

SEI examined the characteristics and concerns of age-defined market segments. This research found that Millennials are not averse to working with financial advisors, but are skeptical of financial institutions. They are always connected with digital technology and social media. In fact, they treat their multitasking handheld devices as a part of their body.[11]

---

[10] "Financial Advisor-Phobia: 71 Percent of Americans Say They Are Scared of Talking to a Financial Advisor," October 27, 2015, www.marketwired.com/press-release/financial-advisor-phobia-71-percent-americans-say-they-are-scared-talking-financial-2067524 .htm.
[11] "Financial Planning Next Wave," SEI *Annual Planning Report,* April 2015.

Millennials have a number of concerns. Their major concern is financing their children's education. They are almost as concerned about the possibility of another financial crisis and building savings that will last through retirement. Most are concerned about student loan debt. Surprisingly, they are *more* risk-averse than older Baby Boomers.

The challenge facing financial advisors is to help these Millennials become more comfortable with investing. One approach is the increased promotion of mobile apps that help them with money management. Jay attended the Finnovate event in London in early 2015. The event showcased 70 new financial technology companies or ideas. Seventy presenters were each given seven minutes to discuss their companies or ideas and were expected to conduct a live demo. Out of the 70 companies that made presentations, almost one in four of the ideas presented dealt with simplifying budgeting, saving, and mobile payments. The apps and ideas were designed to encourage saving and investing.

Yes, there's a lot of noise out there, but much of it is just that— noise. If, as an advisory community, we focus on simplifying the client's life, and thereby bringing better outcomes to the client, the probability of a bright future far outweighs the probability of a negative outcome.

 THE CONSUMER PERSPECTIVE

Financial advisors play a role in educating their clients. Although Pam Krueger has done her best to educate consumers with her *MoneyTrack* program, American consumers on the whole are not financially literate. Too many people view investing as boring and over their heads. If you have ever seen the program on your local PBS station, you'll find the average consumer will easily understand the concepts. The program is anything but highbrow, especially when her dog, Chloe, a Labradoodle, walks across the set in the middle of a shot.

Hollywood has tried to make high finance entertaining, but with limited success. In December 2015, the movie *The Big Short* was released. The film was based on Michael Lewis's best-seller, which had the same name. The movie did its best to explain how mortgage loans were packaged into mortgage-backed securities (MBS). The movie showed behavioral economist Richard Thaler and singer Selena Gomez at a blackjack table in an effort to explain derivatives. Actress Margot Robbie explained why banks began filling MBS with riskier mortgages while taking a bubble bath. Actor Ryan Gosling played a trader for

Deutsche Bank who uses a tower of toy Jenga blocks to illustrate how securities were sliced into *tranches*, the French word for slice. In the investment world, the term refers to a security that can be sliced into smaller parts and sold to investors.[12]

The Big Short is not the first time Hollywood has worked diligently to make the financial world look exciting. Movies like *Wolf of Wall Street*, *Wall Street*, and *Too Big to Fail* were valiant attempts to educate and entertain audiences about the seamy side of investing.

Michael Spellacy, the global wealth management leader at PricewaterhouseCoopers, has stated that robo investing can help improve client financial literacy. Investors can see how their assets are allocated based on their goals, as well as how portfolios are rebalanced over time and changing circumstances. Robo technologies, according to Spellacy, can provide a crash course in portfolio optimization and can help investors understand the tribal language of investing.[13]

Spellacy contended that as younger investors become more financially literate and build their asset bases, they will inevitably gain greater appetites for more professional guidance. With greater literacy, investors of any age will gain an enhanced comprehension of financial advice and their investment options. As a result, they will feel more engaged with their advisors.

One of the key points of our book is quite simple. The best firms are going to be able to differentiate what they do from the others and show consumers the difference. Sounds simple, doesn't it? However, let's flip the table and not look at the situation as industry professionals. Instead, let's look at it through the eyes of the consumer. Here are some exercises for advisors to work through to see how consumers view them. These exercises are based on my interaction with thousands of consumers who were searching for financial advice.

EXERCISE 1: YOU ALL SOUND THE SAME

The first exercise is called, "You All Sound the Same." Here's what happens when consumers are looking for financial advice: they get on the Internet and begin searching. They come across four randomly

---

[12] Greg Ip, "What 'The Big Short' Got Right and Wrong," *Wall Street Journal*, December 12–13, 2015, B5.

[13] Michael Spellacy, "Robo-Advisors Can Have a Positive Influence on Clients' Financial Literacy," December 14, 2015, www.investmentnews.com/article/20151214/BLOG09/151219965/robo-advisers-can-have-a-positive-influence-on-clients-financial.

selected firms, each with its own value proposition. The following list includes those four value statements, and a consumer's potential reaction to each one:

1. *As a nationally recognized leader in the wealth management community, we are focused on providing clients with customized investment plans and comprehensive wealth management services.*

   At XYZ Firm, we believe a client's portfolio must take into account where they are and where they want to go, as well as all of the unique circumstances that apply to their situations. For over 30 years, we have been working with individuals and institutions to customize and manage portfolios designed to optimize the probability of success.

   "Nationally recognized" certainly sounds impressive, but consumers will wonder what it really means and how it matters to them. Remember, Bernie Madoff and his Ponzi scheme were nationally recognized, so it's important to provide context to support a vague claim like this (e.g., an award from a respected consumer advocacy or industry group). Even better, avoid these kinds of stock phrases.

   A customized, comprehensive approach should make clients and prospects feel they are being viewed as individuals, not assets on which the advisor will make a fee. Using this language is a promise that firms need to make good on.

   Many consumers will like the idea of customized advice and will expect advisors to explain why a particular portfolio approach will help them reach their goals. The term "comprehensive wealth management" is often thrown around by advisory firms even though it feels empty to many consumers. It will leave them wondering if they will get advice about every aspect of their financial well-being or only those issues they bring to an advisor's attention.

2. *At XYZ Firm, we help clients to create an investment plan and financial plan that is flexible enough to meet unexpected challenges—yet disciplined enough to maintain their long-term vision for the future.*

We employ a conservative, balanced, and disciplined approach to investing that aims to help you meet your goals while minimizing your risk. We believe that the best way to achieve this outcome is to make sure that your portfolio reflects the right mix of asset classes as well as the optimal selection of individual securities. Four main tenets underpin our investment approach: personalized service, disciplined portfolio construction, rigorous oversight, and detailed reporting.

Consumers appreciate candor and straight talk from their advisors. They understand that even though the firm attempts to construct an optimal portfolio, they still might lose money—and they want advisors to be up front about this possibility.

One advisor says there will be an optimal selection of individual securities for my portfolio, while a firm down the block says the same thing, but offers very different securities. Consumers want to understand the logic and strategy behind a recommended asset allocation. This is much more important than a guarantee that things will be fine during the next bear market. An advisor should provide a range of anticipated profits and losses during various economic climates, and the conversation about what to include in a portfolio should flow two ways.

3. *Our disciplined and comprehensive wealth management services include taking into account your entire financial picture to provide financial planning, asset allocation, cash flow analysis, and tax-sensitive investing overlay. We combine these holistic services with our attention to building strong, secure client-advisor relationships.*

Advisors believe investors understand the word "holistic." When they tout their holistic financial planning approaches, it might go over the prospect's head. A prospect might think it's a spiritual approach to financial planning.

Millennials are focused more on cash flow than other age groups. Clients of any age will raise holy hell if the advisor's holistic services leave them scrimping to get by and force drastic changes in their lifestyle.

4. *Founded in 19XX, XYZ is an independent, fee-only investment advisor providing customized portfolio management services and comprehensive financial planning solutions to each family's unique financial situation.*

Consumers know they don't want cookie-cutter financial plans from advisors. They like being told their financial situations are unique, even if many of their consumer brethren face the same problems. Comprehensive financial planning is not always as comprehensive as clients and prospects expect. The comprehensive financial plan should address every aspect of the client's financial well-being.

Many advisors who brag about their comprehensive financial planning never get around to discussing funeral planning. Liz Skinner, a reporter for InvestmentNews, wrote that it makes sense for advisors to bring up the idea of funeral planning during discussions of estate planning or insurance. Funeral and burial costs range from $10,000 to $30,000. The discussion gives clients the opportunity to express their wishes from major decisions like burial preferences, to less ground-breaking choices such as receptions, viewings, services, and newspaper obituaries, which can cost $1,000 to $1,500 per publication.[14]

EXERCISE 2: PRESENTATION IS EVERYTHING

If you are an advisor, take a minute to think about the investments you are recommending to clients. Will your discussions go over the client or prospect's head? Are you worried that if your recommendations are too simplistic, the client or prospect will not think you're providing value? On the other hand, are you touting complex investment products like derivatives or alternative asset classes? Can you explain the product in language that an unsophisticated investor can understand?

I know of at least one advisor who recommends very sophisticated financial products to clients. His approach is rather patronizing. The advisor pats clients on the hands and tells them this product will help them reach their goals, even though they won't be able to understand why.

---

[14] Liz Skinner, "Advisers Help Plan for Taxes, and Some for the Other Sure Thing in Life: Death," *Investment News*, December 8, 2015, www.investmentnews.com/article/20151208/FREE/151209928/advisers-help-plan-for-taxes-and-some-for-the-other-sure-thing-in.

Discussions with consumers should not be designed to show consumers how smart an advisor is. If they leave the office befuddled, consumers are not likely to sign an advisory agreement.

As advisors craft their value propositions, they sometimes use language that does not resonate with investors. For example, advisors may describe their firm as "high-touch." The term refers to a business that develops a very close relationship with its customers or clients. A random and nonscientific survey of individuals outside the financial services industry found they were unfamiliar with the term "high-touch." If a prospect does not understand the buzzwords in an advisor's value proposition, it will fall on deaf ears. The phrase "open architecture" is bandied about by advisors without explaining what that means to the average investor.

For the longest time, people used the phrase "walk the talk" and "walk the walk." Advisors can tout that they walk the talk, believing that prospects will know that means they do what they say they are going to do. Unfortunately, clients do not always get these figures of speech that are popular for a while but then fade away. One advisor couched the phrase in user-friendly language: "We do what we say and say what we do."

When advisors discuss the investments they're recommending, they love to use the phrase, "We eat our own cooking." Attempts like these by advisors to use homespun phrases may fall flat with consumers unless the advisor fleshes out the point a bit.

Many advisors use and overuse the word "unique" to describe what differentiates them from other firms. On one financial advisor's website, the firm used the word "unique" ad nauseam to describe its investment approach, people, philosophy, and services. The word "unique" might convey very little to investors because the adjective is so overused. It might cause a securities examiner to ask, "How are you unique and can you prove it with objective evidence?"

An advisor's value proposition must be grounded in reality. One advisor's marketing pitch implied that investors should choose his firm if their goal was to retire in their forties, buy a beach home, and travel the world. Individuals reading his advertisement could infer they would be able to achieve all of those goals by hiring him.

KEY TAKEAWAYS

■ The value of advice is driven by an advisor's ability to bring simplicity from the complexity to the end consumer. The complexity of clients' lives is increasing and so is the need for financial advice.

■ It is becoming increasingly more challenging to differentiate your firm's value proposition given the exploding number of choices from which a consumer has to select.

■ The opportunities and challenges of the future will be caused by the bifurcation of those firms that are able to grow and those that cannot. This growth will be based on two key variables: (1) the ability invest in the best talent, and (2) the ability to invest in marketing to differentiate. Both of these investments will require scale.

■ We've created our own complexity. Consumers think most firms sound the same. Be clear about what makes you different. Ensure it isn't the same as the person down the street.

■ As an industry, we must continue to focus on the *services* part of the financial services title. Thirty-eight percent of the U.S. population isn't currently saving for retirement. The investing public needs financial advice to meet their life goals.

CHAPTER 3

The Digital Divide
Napster or Amazon?

If you're not stubborn, you'll give up on experiments too soon. And if you're not flexible, you'll pound your head against the wall and you won't see a different solution to a problem you're trying to solve.

—Jeff Bezos

A TALE OF TWO COMPANIES

It was 1999, and every technology leader on a college campus in America was shaking their head because server usage was off the charts. What was going on? Napster was going on. For readers who first listened to music on AM radios, vinyl records, eight-track tapes, and cassettes, it will help to give a history of Napster. Napster was a revolutionary way for music lovers to share and listen to their favorite songs. Shawn Fanning and Sean Parker came up with the idea of an online platform where users could swap songs. Napster was launched in June 1999 and its usage quickly spread through the world. By March 2000, 20 million people used Napster. Millions more began using it in the months that followed.[1] All they needed was a computer and a dial-up connection. The platform enabled people to share audio files and, because the Internet was so slow, it would sometimes take 15 minutes or more to download one song. The final frustration could come if a user realized he or she had downloaded the wrong version.

Napster users fell in love with the online platform. After years of going to brick-and-mortar stores to buy CDs, music lovers could have their favorite songs for *free*. There was no need to sit by the radio with a tape recorder and wait for a song to be played, and no one worried about buying a whole album to get the one good song that wasn't released as a single. At the time, in 1999, a top-100 album was $13.65. To put that price into perspective, a share of Apple stock cost a little over $100 at that time, and an ounce of gold was little less than $300. The average monthly cellphone bill was $40.24.[2]

The throngs of people flocking to Napster soon attracted the attention of the Recording Industry Association of America (RIAA), which represents recording artists and record labels. The RIAA and many musicians viewed folks at Napster as thieves who were undermining their business. There were, however, some musicians who felt that Napster gave them exposure they would not have received through other means. During that time period, if you were under the age of 25, you had an opinion of Napster—and you most likely thought it was changing the world for the better.

Just a few years before the start of Napster, entrepreneur Jeff Bezos founded Amazon, a retail company he ran from his garage. In 1997, Amazon went public for $18 per share. Much of this value came from how Amazon was disrupting retail sales, which happened in much the same way Napster was disrupting the music industry. In 1999, Jeff Bezos was named the *Time* magazine's Person of the Year for making Internet shopping a household norm.

Today, Amazon is expected to reap annual revenues in excess of $60 billion, and Napster is out of business. You might ask what

[1] Alex Suskind, "15 Years after Napster: How the Music Service Changed the Industry," *The Daily Beast*, June 6, 2014, www.thedailybeast.com/articles/2014/06/06/15-years-after-napster-how-the-music-service-changed-the-industry.html.

[2] Tom Barlow, "Then vs. Now: How Prices Have Changed since 1999," *Daily Finance*, December 30, 2009, www.dailyfinance.com/2009/12/29/then-vs-now-how-prices-have-changed-since-1999/.

happened and what in the world does this have to do with financial services? Those are two very important questions, and the answers give us the roadmap to the future in financial services.

According to History.com, Napster's downfall began on March 6, 2001, the date on which it began complying with a federal court order blocking the transfer of copyrighted material over its peer-to-peer network:

> Oh, but people enjoyed it while it lasted. At the peak of Napster's popularity in late 2000 and early 2001, some 60 million users around the world were freely exchanging digital mp3 files with the help of the program developed by Northeastern University college student Shawn Fanning in the summer of 1999. Radiohead? Robert Johnson? The Runaways? Metallica? Nearly all of their music was right at your fingertips, and free for the taking. Which, of course, was a problem for the bands, like Metallica, which after discovering their song "I Disappear" circulating through Napster prior to its official release, filed suit against the company, alleging "vicarious copyright infringement" under the U.S. Digital Millennium Copyright Act of 1996.[3]

Metallica's lawsuit was followed by a copyright infringement case brought by hip-hop artist, Dr. Dre. The kiss of death, however, was RIAA's $20 billion lawsuit.

Despite its end in 2002, Napster is still ingrained in our culture. The Napster brand and logos were acquired following the company's bankruptcy, and its founders have been portrayed in movies ranging from *The Social Network* to the remake of *The Italian Job*. Currently, Napster is part of Rhapsody's music streaming service, but it will be most remembered as a tech upstart that changed the way people think about music.

THE FATE OF ROBO ADVISORS

Both Napster and Amazon were disruptive—they changed the game in their respective industries. By way of comparison, we are still in the initial stages of a financial digital revolution. Questions remain as

---

[3] "The Death Spiral of Napster Begins," History.com, www.history.com/this-day-in-history/the-death-spiral-of-napster-begins.

to whether the robo movement will prove to be like Napster, which didn't have staying power, or like Amazon, which permanently disrupted an entire business model.

If you talk with the early adopters of Napster, you will find many of the industry experts back then missed the point. They believed that the early success of Napster stemmed from the fact that the music was free. Jay was an early adopter of Napster and believes this opinion misses the mark. Price was only a small part of the value equation. The distribution model changes were what made the use of Napster attractive. Being able to get any song you wanted on your computer in 15 minutes was unbelievable. In the end, Apple took the Napster concept onto a real business platform, charging for downloads, which shows it wasn't all about price. While Amazon took many years to make money, it exists today, and dominates retail shopping. Not only is it disruptive but, more importantly, it is a real business.

The new disruptors of the financial industry are robo advisors, investment platforms that use algorithms to automate portfolio management. For all the fanfare these services have received in the past few years, the reality is they are more like Napster than Amazon. We have believed this for years. As we were finishing the final draft of this book, our predictions began coming to fruition. The robo advisors that came on the scene early in the digital movement will likely not continue as stand-alone companies because their business models are broken.

Morningstar and other research organizations have estimated the robo advisors would need to service somewhere between $30 billion and $40 billion in assets to break even when charging 25 basis points for services. Even the top stand-alone robo advisors have not reached $10 billion, so the proposition of getting to $30 billion is daunting. We believe these break-even amounts also do not take into account the growing expenditures these organizations will need to make to offer more services than they currently provide. The digital experience isn't holding up on its own. The investments these early robo advisors are now making in call centers and virtual planning will make providing these services for 25 basis points impossible. These companies have been built on the large investments from venture and private equity firms. How long will these investors continue to invest?

The acquisition of many of the early adopting robo advisors by traditional financial services firms shows the robo movement is not a stand-alone company concept. Just look at the number of transactions that occurred in 2015 alone: Blackrock acquired Future Advisor; Northwestern Mutual Insurance Company bought Learnvest; and we at Envestnet purchased Upside. In December of 2015, it was reported by InvestmentNews and other media outlets that Personal Capital had hired an investment banker to find a buyer.[4] Personal Capital is a hybrid digital advisor, which has spent $112 million to attract $1.5 billion in assets under management. There's a lot of capital in the market and someone will buy them, but the ability to sustain those economics on the long term as a stand-alone firm is likely impossible.

FROM CHANNEL TO SOLUTION

In the early stages of the robo-advisor movement, the financial services media and industry veterans didn't know what category to put these new business models in, so many of them considered categorizing these new robo organizations in a separate channel. Wealthfront came on the scene and focused on attracting affluent Silicon Valley Millennials. Consequently, Wealthfront was put into the category to compete against traditional financial and wealth management advice. As such, this had to be a new channel, right? Over time, you would then put banks, broker-dealers, registered investment advisors (RIAs), and robo advisors in separate categories that were all competing for the same prospects. See Figure 3.1.

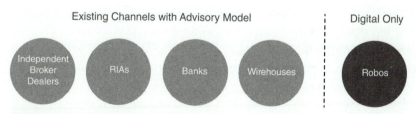

Figure 3.1 The Wrong View of Digital

---

[4] Alessandra Malito, "Personal Capital Hires Investment Bank to Find Buyer, Funding—peHUB," *InvestmentNews*, December 10, 2015, www.investmentnews.com/article/20151210/FREE/151219991/personal-capital-hires-investment-bank-to-find-buyer-funding-pehub.

However, as the industry stands today, other than Wealthfront, which is still a stand-alone robo advisor focused solely on the retail market, the robo movement has changed from a channel to a supporting tool for traditional advice models. The robo movement and its technology, much like Napster, has shown there is a new way for traditional service models to morph into new distribution patterns better positioned to meet end-client needs. Later in this chapter, we will discuss what we believe will be the lasting impact of the robo-advisor movement. One of the most significant impacts is the new business models the movement has brought to the industry. As an industry, one of our greatest challenges has been our inability to effectively serve a wider and smaller client base. The robo movement may provide a roadmap to resolving this issue. As the robo-advisor movement morphs into a digital movement combined with traditional business models, digital technology is helping us overcome the challenge of providing financial advice to a wider client base that has less money to invest. The future of digital is depicted in Figure 3.2.

Digital technology platforms combined with traditional models are going to help banks and wirehouses serve smaller accounts. Hopefully, a wider subset of the population will be able to receive intelligent financial advice, allowing for better financial decisions. Many RIAs are focused on planning and doing sophisticated planning for higher-end clients. The data aggregation capabilities of the new digital platforms

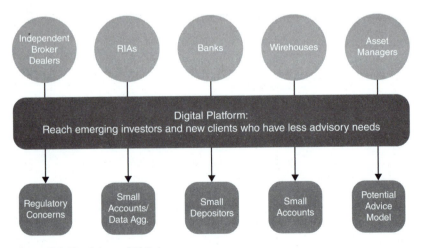

Figure 3.2 The Future of Digital

will allow advisors to provide better planning advice as information and transparency is easier to reach.

Regulators have the potential to drastically change the asset management community, especially directly held mutual fund companies and asset managers. The digital platforms of today and into the future will allow asset managers and mutual fund companies to efficiently serve their clients as the burden of regulation rises. As the robo movement began, some advisors were singing along to that R.E.M. song "It's the End of the World as We Know It." However, in an ironic twist, the robo advisors have created technologies and focused our industry on the way forward to bring better service and outcomes to consumers.

We believe there will be a surprise ending to the robo-advisor movement that is every bit as shocking as the final moments of the movie *The Usual Suspects*. (We won't spoil it for you here.) The technology underlying those platforms, which was feared by so many people in the financial services industry, has actually brought us the solutions we were searching for to help investors with smaller portfolios. Furthermore, robo advisors will help bring investment advice to individuals who do not have enough assets to warrant the hiring of a traditional advisor. In many ways, this group needs financial advice far more than wealthier investors.

THE LASTING IMPACT OF ROBOS

When we speak at client and industry events, someone in the crowd almost always asks something like this: "Do you think the robo advisors are going to be disruptive to the industry and to human advisors?" Everyone has a different answer. We try to give you our thoughts and the thoughts of those collaborating with us on this project. The goal is not to be too academic in this book, but humor us for a second because we think the definition of "disruption" is important to the answer. According to Dictionary.com, the relevant definition for this conversation is: "a radical change in an industry, business strategy, etc., especially involving the introduction of a new product or service that creates a new market." Even when you look at this definition, it is unclear if the robo advisors created a new market. It is also difficult to determine whether they are truly replacing a current model.

Michael Kitces doesn't believe the robo movement is disruptive. "One or two robos surviving as stand-alone entities, just by definition isn't disruptive." Kitces's point is that disruption is defined by the survival of the actual robo entities. In talking with Michael, his beliefs are in line with ours. The argument about whether the robos are disruptive is really an academic exercise that is unimportant and poses the wrong question. The right question to ask is: has the robo movement changed how advisors need to operate and will it leave a lasting legacy? The answer is a resounding *yes*. Based on what robo advisors have brought so far, we believe there will be many ways the trend will leave its legacy.

New Tools

Kitces believes the biggest lasting impact of the robo advisors is the fact that the new entrants to the market showed the industry how embarrassing our client facing technology was:

> As an industry, we became very myopic. Even the early adopters of client technology rested on their laurels. They looked at everybody else around them and felt they were light years ahead. They were light years ahead compared to that population, but not to other industries when the consumer compared the financial services industry to everyone else they do business with on a daily basis.

The average consumer is exposed to sleek, well-functioning technology that easily integrates into daily life. The financial industry does have additional hurdles that come in the form of security and regulation, but having strong digital tools is absolutely necessary. Robo advisors were able to figure this out and appeal to consumers in this regard.

Valuation

Robo advisors put specific prices on services related to asset allocation, investment vehicle selection, and systematic rebalancing, and offered them all as part of the value chain. As the market begins to agree on value for those services, advisors will be able to differentiate and set prices more easily—and it's possible robo advisors will have set the price floor. They will also be able to present a strong value proposition as it relates to the core components of financial advice. Consumers will also be able to better choose between competitors by comparing their price, performance, and level of service.

Data Aggregation

The belief that consumers want to see their entire financial life in one place really goes all the way back to 1980 when Merrill Lynch launched cash management accounts. It was a way to combine bank and brokerage accounts, thus consolidating the assets and cash into one statement, allowing a customer to see their relationship value in one place. At Envestnet, we've been focused on this for a long time, but have noted it's only become extremely important to the end consumer in the past couple of years and that trend is continuing. It's one of the reasons we spent around $590 million to acquire Yodlee, a data aggregation company.

We believe the robo advisor players were the ones that accelerated the aggregation trend. Now many consumers, working on digital personal advice platforms, cannot imagine life without seeing all of their assets and liabilities in one place. Imagine the clarity this provides. The client-advisor relationship can function much more effectively when an advisor is privy to a client's complete financial picture. The ability to provide this comprehensive snapshot not only provides a valuable service to the consumer, but it gives the advisor a clear picture on which to base recommendations and strategy. If you're a football fan, you've seen a quarterback look at aerial pictures of the defense sent by a coach who is sitting up in the booth high above the stadium. Just as those photos help the quarterback and the coach decide which plays to call, a financial snapshot helps an advisor determine what strategies are the right call for a client.

Consumer Education

How many investors knew what systematic rebalancing was three years ago? Not many. How many know what systematic rebalancing is today? It's impossible to know exactly how many, but we know for a fact this number has grown as a result of the robo-advisor movement. As the digital movement progresses and continues, consumers are going to want to be more a part of the decision-making process. *This is going to create a major opportunity for those firms that excel in client education.* This is important to really grasp and is a concept we argued over as we drafted the book. Most older clients today come from a position where they don't want to be educated. They want advisors to make decisions for them. Younger clients and prospects view the world differently. They expect to have a seat at the table. They expect to be educated on the recommendations made on their behalf. For most advisors this is a very good thing. Clients who better understand the industry and the difference between good and bad services will presumably gravitate to better advisors.

Cost, Not Value

The robo movement has gained so much traction, in large part, because these newcomers have exploited people's desire for low *costs*. This has caused consumers to focus on cost instead of *value*. What the robo advisors have done is to drive down the cost of implementation and overhead, which has made investing more affordable. However, robo advisors have only selected a few items in the value chain to support their argument that they are less expensive.

Throughout the remainder of the book, we will explore how traditional advisors are going to need to bring consumers' focus back to value. That is where robo advisors find it difficult to compete. Keep in mind that advising is a *service* industry, and automated portfolio platforms find it very hard to compete in this regard.

A Definition of "Advice"

The final lasting legacy of the stand-alone robo movement is the window it provides for the human advisor to differentiate what true advice looks like. The remainder of our book will focus on the value equation of the future for the human advisor and how firms need to build upon this value equation. We believe there's a difference between data, insights, and advice. Moreover, we believe the digital platforms of the future will provide the data and the insights and the human advisor will interpret these and provide them to the end consumer. This ability to show how advice impacts client lives is what Dow Chemical Company calls the "Human Element."

Amazon.com permanently disrupted the retail sector. It has become the go-to place for many consumers to buy just about every kind of product, not just books. Similarly, online travel websites certainly cut into the profits of travel agents. Nevertheless, just as tax preparation software did not eliminate the need for accountants, robo advisors will not take away the need for human advisors. The stand-alone robo advisors are more like Napster, something temporary that builds the foundation of the future. Human advisors mixed with sophisticated platforms are prepared to disrupt the financial industry at the level of retailer Amazon. Human advisors who can add sufficient value will continue to thrive despite the influx of robos and automated investment tools.

 ## THE CONSUMER PERSPECTIVE

Previous sections have discussed the trust gap between the consumer and the financial services industry. Pam Krueger encounters it all the time in her work with consumers. This gap is real and the idea of the robo advisor plays into this fear. For so long, investors have felt like they weren't empowered, like they didn't have the ability to do anything on their own. Day trading or stock picking were available, but that isn't appealing to most consumers. It seems too complicated.

Suddenly, like Napster, the robo advisors come along and they make the whole experience feel simple. Everyday investors now feel empowered—as though they're in partnership with someone they can trust. This empowerment is real, yet often overlooked by both consumers and advisors. The digital movement, one where digital technology comes together with the human advisor, has the capability of making the consumer feel equally as empowered if done properly.

The thing to worry most about for consumers who rely on the digital-only solutions is creating a false sense of security. We see this as an issue because consumers *want to believe* there's someone watching out to protect them, and we know consumers are often way off the mark when they try to accurately describe their own financial circumstances. Although most consumers don't have the time or the interest in paying

(*Continued*)

(*Continued*)

attention to the regulators, it is interesting to note that the SEC publishes Investor Alerts when the Commission believes investors are at risk. On May 8, 2015, the SEC made the following observations about automated investment tools:

> At the swipe of a fingertip on a mobile device or the click of a mouse on a desktop computer, investors can access a broad range of automated investment tools. These tools range from personal financial planning tools (such as online calculators) to portfolio selection or asset optimization services (such as services that provide recommendations on how to allocate your 401(k) or brokerage account) to online investment management programs (such as robo-advisors that select and manage investment portfolios).

> Many financial professionals have used automated investment tools for decades to help customers build and manage their investment portfolios, and a growing number of these tools are now available directly to investors from a variety of sources. While automated investment tools may offer clear benefits—including low cost, ease of use, and broad access—it is important to understand their risks and limitations before using them. Investors should be wary of tools that promise better portfolio performance.[5]

While a later chapter will fully cover fees, it is interesting the way Charles Schwab originally marketed their Schwab Intelligent Portfolios. The original commercials described the advice as *free*. Obviously it's not free because Schwab is compensated for the investments that are created by them and end up in the packaged solutions. Investors should understand any terms and conditions associated with the automated investment tool. For example, there may be fees and expenses that arise when using the tool or selling or purchasing investments. Investors should ask if the investment tool sponsor receives any form of compensation for offering, recommending, or selling certain services or investments.

Another reason why the robo-advisor movement is Napster and not Amazon is the burden it requires for consumers to consider the tool's limitations, including the assumptions on which it is based. An automated investment tool may be programmed to rely on economic assumptions that will not react to shifts in the market. As the old expression goes, *garbage in, garbage out*. An automated tool's output directly depends on what information it seeks from the investor and the information provided. If the questions asked are not precise, the recommendations generated will be suspect. Consumers don't fully understand this and the advisory community can help with this education point.

---

[5] "Investor Alert: Automated Investment Tools," U.S. Securities and Exchange Commission, May 8, 2015, www.sec.gov/oiea/investor-alerts-bulletins/autolistingtoolshtm.html.

The SEC also warned that an automated tool's output may not be right for an investor's financial needs or objectives. It might not consider all of the investor's particular circumstances, such as age, financial situation and needs, investment experience, other holdings, tax situation, willingness to risk losing your investment money for potentially higher investment returns, time horizon for investing, need for cash, and investment goals. The tool might suggest investments, including asset allocation models, which are inappropriate for an investor. The investor's time horizon may be based exclusively on age. It might not take into consideration the fact that an investor has an event like a wedding to pay for in a few years.

In the end, a consumer relying on digital only "advice" really is taking on a lot more decision responsibility than many assume. The automated investment tools are programmed to generate outputs, but in the end, consumers are left to themselves to decide.

KEY TAKEAWAYS

- The lasting impact of the digital movement is its simplification of the client experience. The human advisor must embrace this simplicity in the future.

- The early digital movement companies will not be long-lasting as stand-alone companies. The early digital providers will ultimately morph into traditional distribution channels.

- The digital movement has the ability to engage consumers and bring them over the trust gap. If we as an industry can minimize this trust gap, a major opportunity to grow practices and widen advisor impact exists.

- The digital movement, like Napster, is playing out as a major change to the financial services industry, but human advisors who embrace the benefits will lead the way to the next iteration of financial advice.

- The digital movement has allowed consumers to feel empowered. This is a positive thing for the end consumer. However, this empowerment may be creating a false sense of security if the consumer is not careful.

CHAPTER 4

The Pillars
of Value

I used to pride myself on being the first in the office in the morning and one of the last to leave at night. Now, that's so dated: It's not about effort, it's about outcomes.

—Maynard Webb

Have you ever wondered what it must be like to be a comedian? You spend hours rehearsing what you think are wonderful jokes. The jokes are witty. Your delivery is going to be perfectly timed. When you finally take the stage, the lights are bright and hot. You are completely prepared, and you tell the first joke only to receive no laughter. Standing on stage, you think of *Ferris Bueller's Day Off* and channel your inner Ben Stein. You tap the microphone and say: "Bueller . . . Bueller . . ." The attempt to save the joke, which is now on life support, fails miserably.

Thinking that the audience was the problem, you try again the next night, only to fail again. How disheartening. Similarly, without a proactive approach to defining value in the relationship with clients, we believe some advisors run the risk of falling flat on stage.

Although we are taking the longer view here, we believe the value proposition of many advisors in the industry will need to be communicated and built differently as the industry changes. The outside pressures, which encompass everything from Department of Labor and SEC regulations, as well as the changing technology landscape, will cause advisors to think long and hard about the value proposition that will deliver client value in the future.

Let's begin the determination of value by starting at its most important component: the client. The client has a need for financial advice. These needs vary client by client. The advisor can meet those needs, but how do advisors and clients even assess what is needed and where there is value?

We started this chapter talking about comedians, but what is no laughing matter is the compliance statements required to set the correct expectations for the readers of this chapter: *This chapter does not represent nor does it intend to represent financial, legal, or tax advice. Anyone seeking financial advice should seek the services of a professional. Any comments about investment vehicles are based on historical research. Past performance is not an indicator of future performance.*

DEFINING VALUE—A LARGE BROADER VIEW

An ongoing debate among investment advisors and their clients centers on value: creating it, preserving it, and perpetuating it. Advisors are tasked with delivering worth to their clients, and clients need to understand what they can expect for the dollars they spend.

This chapter is extremely important to set up the remainder of the book. Some quantitative research at this point in the discussion is relevant and important. For those readers not interested in a deep dive of quantitative research, we tried to structure the chapter to make it easier to digest. The summary is designed to provide a higher-level perspective of the value framework. We then go deeper on each pillar of value for those wishing to dig deep in calculating the basis point values we discuss in the summary, which we will explain shortly.

If advisors cannot begin to articulate and quantify where value can be added to the end consumer, how can they articulate a value proposition, operate their firms against this value and, what may be most important, justify fees charged? If you are an end consumer, understanding what's important to your relationship with an advisor and the value an advisor can bring is a key bridge to understanding the advisor's value proposition.

Over the past three years at Envestnet, we have spent significant time and resources researching, defining, and quantifying the areas where we believe an advisor provides value to an end consumer. We call this research Capital Sigma. This term is used to represent the sum total of advisor-created value. You will hear us talking throughout the remainder of the book about the pillars of value. The pillars of value are the five areas where we determined an advisor can provide value. These five pillars of value are depicted in Figure 4.1.

We will start with a high-level review of our findings and then dig deeper into each of the five. Each element can generate a benefit *alpha*, or excess return over a given benchmark—the traditional mark of gauging success. Our research shows advisors, when they successfully implement the five core areas of value, can deliver excess value of up to 3 percent per year for their clients. To be clear this is *not* what the advisor is charging, it is the potential value the advisor can create for the end consumer. We will explain each value area, and assign a figure to quantify the value it generates. Some may argue with the research in this study. Some may argue it's just like any other study completed in the industry by Vanguard, Morningstar, or others. However, as you will see throughout this chapter, we not only completed the academic research, but we have been able to test many of the figures using the primary data from the 42,000 advisors on Envestnet's platform. By analyzing the performance of these advisors and the accounts they serve, we have been able to show how actual behavior and results compare to the research in Capital Sigma. (The time period of the study was September 30, 1996, through June 30, 2014.)

Figure 4.1 The Five Pillars of Advisor-Created Value

A SUMMARY OF VALUE CREATION

The first pillar of value, *financial planning*, starts with a deep dive into understanding who the client is and what he or she seeks to accomplish. When properly grounded in trust and transparency, it serves as the roadmap to achieving the client's goals ranging from short-term income needs and extending to estate planning and philanthropy. Knowing your client is more than a regulatory hurdle. Rather, it is the first link in the advisor value chain and, when done properly, can result in a winning partnership that procures solid results. Although the value of financial planning derives mostly from its qualitative nature, its all-important role in serving as the cornerstone for the subsequent parts of the advisor-client relationship must be considered in the value equation. Many academic studies have been completed and they have found it difficult to quantify the exact benefit of financial planning and coaching. *We have found a way to quantify the benefits of financial planning and coaching*, and we will discuss this later in the chapter.

The second pillar of advisor-added value is based on crafting an appropriate *asset class selection and asset allocation* through a portfolio strategy that positions the client to achieve her goals. The process begins with determining the proper level of portfolio risk to suit her comfort level, an exercise performed in the financial planning stage, as outlined above. That decision then drives asset class selection. Modeling a suitable asset allocation harnesses both diversification and exposure to a range of investments that can deliver value across a complete market cycle. It also combines a sophisticated institutional methodology that can be tailored to meet a client's personal objectives. That approach may include alternative asset classes, strategic portfolio tilts that apply over- or underweights to capitalize on pricing anomalies, and an array of risk mitigation techniques to respond to changing capital markets and economic conditions.

Once the asset allocation is set, the advisor is tasked with choosing how best to implement it through *investment vehicle selection*, that is, which specific investments he should select to create a customized portfolio for his client. This constitutes the third pillar of advisor-added value. Active asset class managers need to generate excess returns over benchmark to justify their fees, and methods exist to measure how these managers perform. On the passive side, tracking error, portfolio liquidity, and delivery of cost-efficient beta are among the issues the advisor needs to consider in his investment selection process. Our research has determined that employing a strategy of selecting active mutual fund managers according to certain risk-adjusted return characteristics can add value annually to a diversified portfolio, and implementing the portfolio with passive investments can also add value each year.

The fourth pillar of advisor-added value arises from *systematic portfolio rebalancing.* Capital Sigma research demonstrates the advantages of regular, systematic rebalancing and how it can help both to control risk by reducing portfolio volatility and also enhance returns. We contrast the effects of more and less frequent rebalancing and offer a rationale to explain why an annual rebalancing frequency is optimal. The process of systematically rebalancing a diversified portfolio annually can add value each year compared to a naïve strategy of rebalancing once every three years.

The fifth and final pillar of advisor-added value to the client is *tax management.* Although various tax optimization methods and applications exist in the tax management section, we will focus on the potential after-tax benefits an investor can achieve from informed tax management in an all-equity portfolio. A good starting point from a tax efficiency perspective is a buy-and-hold portfolio. However, it does not accommodate offsetting realized capital gains outside the portfolio, the heart of the "tax-loss harvesting" approach to tax optimization. Also, it takes considerable quantitative skill to build a portfolio that tracks a benchmark when only a fraction of that benchmark's holdings can be used. We demonstrate how a sophisticated tracking portfolio that can track a benchmark and accommodate tax harvesting can add considerable after-tax value.

We believe the potential value creation opportunity for end consumers in a relationship with an advisor can be quantified in terms of basis points. For our readers who are consumers, a basis point is one hundredth of 1 percent. Therefore, 28 basis points is a little bit more than a quarter of 1 percent. Figure 4.2 illustrates the potential value of each of the five pillars.

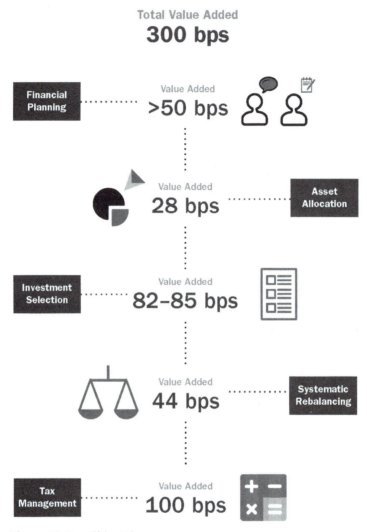

Figure 4.2 Quantifying Value

Let's dig into the numbers.

PILLAR 1: FINANCIAL PLANNING—50+ BASIS POINTS

Long before Google Maps or GPS systems, there was a thing from AAA called a TripTik (they still exist today). It was a small bound map personalized to your vacation destination. You would make an appointment to stop into a local AAA location and you would sit down with a representative to plan your route and learn about potential construction pitfalls and detours. The process of getting a TripTik could be tedious, but because there was really no other customized way to determine your route on a longer trip, it was beneficial. The financial planning process in the past could be equally as tedious and important, so streamlining it and getting consumers to follow the road not only serves as an important outcome for the consumer, but it's also the most important part of the advisory relationship. It seems the pillar of financial planning is the hottest topic in the financial services industry today and ironically the least understood and least uniform. It's one of the major reasons why Fidelity paid $250 million to acquire eMoney, and why Envestnet purchased Finance Logix.

Don't get Michael Kitces started on the value financial planning can bring to the consumer relationship:

> Of course planning brings significant value, but imagine being the consumer and trying to figure out how much. We don't have a standard definition as an industry around what financial planning is. We don't have an approach that is an industry best practice. We are stuck with the legacy of planning, which was usually done just to have something interesting to show a client to then talk about investments or a product.

The other point Kitces correctly makes is the fact that cash flow is what really matters and much of the historical planning has been driven around trying to use planning to ultimately sell a product. Of course, the plan needs to lead to the implementation of investment strategies, but the plan has to be a means to that component, not an end.

Planning as Coaching

Have you ever had a great coach, either in sports, dance, music, or life in general? If you are lucky enough to have had a great coach, you likely don't remember how they helped you during the good times as much as you remember them for doing something extraordinary when things were tough for you. They made you perform better than you thought you could, and they likely made you stay the course during a losing streak, injury, sickness, or when you just didn't feel like you wanted to continue on. Why not define coaching in the advisory business in the same way? It's needed and it's important and it's something financial planning sets the stage for. Coaching in our industry could be simply defined as removing emotion from the investing process to allow clients to achieve their financial objectives.

Capital Sigma research concluded that a sound financial planning process is one built on five key components: risk tolerance assessment, tax planning, insurance planning, retirement planning, and estate planning. Our approach is to subdivide retirement planning to include social security planning, life plan coaching, and also what we believe is now the most important and challenging part of the planning process: modeling and assisting with health costs and choices.

Our Capital Sigma research determined that financial planning can deliver *more than 50 basis points of value*, but we struggled to quantify it completely, hindered by the fact that quantifying coaching is a difficult part of the process. Since the completion of the research, we've identified using our platform data, a way to define and quantify the financial planning and coaching aspects of an advisor and consumer relationship. We believe a well-designed financial plan should ultimately lead to an investment solution. That investment solution, of course, may change over the life of the planning cycle, but the value of the plan is setting a road map and an agreement up front on the objectives and staying the course on the road to successful completion of those objectives.

The best way for clients to reach their goals is to stay invested throughout the long term, ignoring market volatility to invest through an entire market cycle. Human advisors do a lot of therapy sessions with their clients. Frequently, they talk clients off the ledge during periods of market turmoil. Counseling and hand-holding become particularly important during market downturns. Behavioral biases, when left unchecked, can cause clients to act impulsively. These impulsive acts can be detrimental to a client's long-term financial goals. By leveraging the bond forged with clients, an advisor can steer them toward an outcome that is prudent, beneficial, and consistent with their objectives. In the end, these services are far more important than outperforming a benchmark.

We reviewed the behavior of approximately 10,000 advisors running their own investment models on our platform from January 2007 through June 2015, a period in which we would define as a full market cycle: 8.5 years, the market crash of 2008, and a recovery. We compared "strayed to cash" advisors, advisors who went to a cash allocation of greater than 15 percent for a period of greater than three months versus the population of the advisors who stayed in the market. *The advisors who were able to keep their clients in the market outperformed the advisors that didn't by 64 basis points each year over this full market cycle.* A deep financial planning process combined with continuous client coaching does lead to quantifiable value. When a consumer is paying 100 basis points for advice, delivering 64 basis points in planning value goes a long way to making the return on investment work.

PILLAR 2: ASSET CLASS SELECTION AND ALLOCATION—28 BASIS POINTS

We find the vocabulary the industry uses is interesting, and one of the terms we most like to analyze is *investment style*. The word *style* leads to a unique analogy when it comes to an asset class selection or allocation discussion. We all have our own personal fashion styles. When going into a clothing store, most people know what they like and what suits the outcome they are trying to achieve. If I like to wear regular ties then I go to the tie section. If I don't like bow ties because they don't get me to the right style outcome, I avoid the bow tie section. A crucial component of a thoughtfully constructed allocation policy is very similar to our crazy example. An advisor selecting which asset classes to include and the customization of the asset allocation portfolio is rooted in the phase of financial planning when clients and advisors get to know one another. During that phase, advisors assess the clients' particular goals and objectives and determine the appropriate portfolio risk to match their comfort levels. The clients' risk tolerance helps shape the asset allocation mix.

For example, let's turn to Yale University's endowment. Although Yale's endowment office is renowned for its sophisticated asset allocation policy, individual client portfolios may actually be harder to manage. Endowments such as Yale's are typically a single institution portfolio focused on one client. Institutional endowments need not be concerned with tax, retirement, or estate planning constraints. In contrast, financial advisors serve many clients with disparate and ever-evolving needs and objectives, often complicated tax situations, and sometimes intricate retirement and estate planning hurdles. Advisors must apply an institutional mind-set to a personalized and customized asset allocation policy that serves a range of clients.

A thoughtfully developed asset allocation that is diversified and consistent with the client's risk profile and objectives can add *28 basis points of value annually.* Our Capital Sigma research arrived at 28 basis points through an extensive analysis of a basic strategy represented by the Russell 3000 and the Barclays U.S. Aggregate Bond Index against diversified portfolios across three dimensions. We then compare this naïve strategy to one that is diversified across three dimensions. First, we use the same equity/fixed-income split of 56 percent/44 percent represented in both the basic strategy and the world market capitalization portfolios. Second, we diversify within the domestic equity asset class, by establishing multiple combinations, or tiers, of the nine domestic equity styles (i.e., Large Cap, Mid Cap, and Small Cap, each with Value, Core, and Growth components). Finally, we add combinations of nine diversifying asset classes to each domestic equity tier. Among the diversifying asset classes are REITs, International Developed Markets Equity, Emerging Markets Equity, Commodities, High Yield Fixed Income, Global Fixed Income, Treasury Inflation Protected Securities (TIPS), Emerging Market Fixed Income, and Bank Loans. These various combinations result in 6,656 diversified portfolios. We then calculate each portfolio's alpha relative to the naïve strategy over an 18-year period covering December 1996 through December 2014, which is the longest period common to all of the benchmarks we use to represent the various asset classes. The asset allocation alpha relative to the naïve strategy is quite stable across the 6,656 diversified portfolios mentioned above (see Figure 4.2). The proportion of negative alpha diversified portfolios is equal to 0.22, which indicates that approximately four out of five portfolios in the universe of diversified portfolios noted above added positive asset allocation

The asset class selection and allocation process described in this section can be extended to incorporate various risk-mitigating strategies.

For decades, modern portfolio theory (MPT), first introduced by Harry Markowitz in 1952, has been the de facto method for developing diversified asset allocations. The MPT framework includes a host of assumptions, several of which were severely tested in the financial crisis of 2008. One key assumption of MPT is that correlations among asset classes are constant and fixed. However, correlations across asset classes converged. For our nonadvisor readers, when all asset classes move in the same direction, it's a problem. Diversification works in a portfolio because the asset classes tend to move differently across various market outcomes. As one thing is going up, one may be going down in relative value. When every asset class moves in the same direction, diversification in a portfolio no longer provides protection. For this reason, many advisors have embraced supplementing MPT with other risk-mitigating approaches when structuring strategic portfolios, such as tactical overlays or liquid alternatives.

PILLAR 3: INVESTMENT SELECTION—80+ BASIS POINTS

The next step in the process is like buying a car. I know I want an SUV not a sports car. Now do I want heated seats? Do I want a sunroof and four-wheel drive? Once the asset allocation has been crafted from a palette of asset classes, the next step in the advisor value chain is to breathe life into it by selecting the most appropriate investments. These are then knitted together thoughtfully to create a portfolio customized to the client's individual objectives.

Coke or Pepsi? Who shot J. R.? Is Darth Vader really Luke's father? Through the years these have been some of the world's most debated questions. However, these are simple questions compared to the big one: does active management actually provide value? Several studies indicate that, on balance, active management does not generate value over time. Other research concluded that active management can add value in certain asset classes, particularly those that are less efficient. In our Capital Sigma research, we found implementing a portfolio with passive investments can add 82 basis points and active characteristics can add 85 basis points. Again for our potential consumer readers: active strategies trade more often and are designed to outpace a benchmark. The products themselves are more expensive. Passive vehicles are designed to trade less and generally track an index or a benchmark.

Passive products are generally cheaper. The argument on both sides is whether or not active management can outpace additional fees paid.

Active Strategy

Envestnet's strategy for selecting active managers using historical information ratios has several steps. To begin, every quarter we calculate the three-year information ratio for actively managed funds relative to each investment style benchmark. We then combine the data and map it for each investment style into the following primary asset classes: domestic equity, international equity, domestic fixed income, domestic high yield, and international fixed income. The funds in each primary asset class then are ranked by the information ratio and grouped into deciles to measure performance.

The next step is to establish a strategy for selecting active managers. Within each primary asset class, we use the average active return of the top three deciles, as that universe roughly corresponds in percentage terms. We then weight each primary asset class's annual active return by its weight in the world market capitalization portfolio. We then establish a basic benchmark against which to measure the added value of the selection strategy. We use an ETF portfolio as a reasonable benchmark to measure the efficacy of an active manager versus a passive strategy. We assume the active return of each benchmark's primary asset class equals the weighted average expense ratio of the ETFs that comprise it.

Finally we calculate the added value of the active manager selection strategy. We add the annual weighted active return for the active manager selection strategy to the weighted average ETF expense ratio for each primary asset class. This is because you save the ETF expense ratio by *not* adopting the naïve benchmark strategy. We then calculate the alphas, and determine the total value added by the active manager selection strategy: 85 basis points.

Passive Strategy

Calculating the benefits of a passive strategy is a little less complex. In the study, we quantified the added value from implementing a passive portfolio with ETFs because of the popularity of the vehicle in creating passive portfolio solutions. We needed a neutral starting point so we used the world market portfolio as calculated at the end of 2014. We then use Morningstar's peer groups for the various asset classes in the world market portfolio to compute the expected differences in excess return for a median ETF compared to a median active mutual fund. We have made two key assumptions: First, an ETF's excess return compared to its benchmark should be equal to the negative of its expense ratio over time; and second, the expected excess return of an average/median active manager should be equal to the negative of its expense ratio, since the expected alpha of active managers as a whole (here represented by the average/medium active) has to be equal to the negative of their expense ratio. Note that this second assumption does not contradict our value-add assessment of active managers. In that analysis, we focus on a subset of best active managers, which is consistent with average/median managers having expected alpha equal to the negative of their expense ratio. Finally, we aggregate these differences across various asset classes in the world market portfolio to arrive at an overall value add of 82 basis points per year.

PILLAR 4: SYSTEMATIC REBALANCING—44 BASIS POINTS

The next source of the advisor's value contribution is systematic rebalancing. This is the next step in the continuum from financial and investment planning through the strategy's implementation and execution. Advisors make a material and quantifiable contribution to a client's results by establishing a protocol for systematically rebalancing a diversified portfolio, which can add 44 basis points of value annually according to our research. Left to their own devices, investors frequently neglect their asset allocation, and turn their attention to what they perceive to be the more interesting process of monitoring the investment vehicles. Just as the target asset allocation policy is vital to achieving the portfolio's overall investment objective, periodic rebalancing is essential to maintaining its efficacy. Two key benefits arise from a carefully constructed, systematic rebalancing policy:

1. **Greater Risk Control:** Rebalancing preserves the benefits of diversification by mitigating unintended over- or

underexposure to asset classes. Reallocating from more to less volatile ones reduces overall portfolio volatility. It also systematically removes the motion from the decision.

2. **Rebalancing Alpha:** Systematic rebalancing also can enhance returns. Rebalancing takes advantage of the cyclicality of performance trends across asset classes. Is there an optimal frequency for rebalancing? Our research indicates that annual rebalancing generates higher returns than doing so either more or less frequently.

This is another area where we were able to analyze a population of approximately 12,000 advisors on our platform to determine if annually rebalanced accounts outperformed those that were not annually rebalanced from 2010 to June 2015. The accounts that were rebalanced at least once annually throughout that 5.5-year period *outperformed the accounts that were not rebalanced by 53 basis points per year.* The same analysis of the platform data showed *68 percent of accounts in advisor models were not rebalanced* in calendar year 2014, during a time when the equity markets were up double digits. This points to a potential area where advisors are missing an opportunity to provide value to their end clients.

PILLAR 5: TAX MANAGEMENT—100 BASIS POINTS

There's a radio commercial currently playing for a regional car dealership. The message is clever: "If you want to pay more, that's your business. If you want to pay less, that's *our* business." Taxes work much the same way. For the most part, people want to pay less and advisors have the ability to help manage that expectation. The tax management pillar provides the largest value opportunity in hard numbers. Managing an all equity portfolio for tax optimization can add approximately 100 basis points of annual value when compared to an investment strategy that is not actively managed. Although it is difficult to disagree with Benjamin Franklin, who back in 1789 said, "In this world nothing can be said to be certain, except death and taxes," too often the implications stemming from this statement are ignored in the world of investing. Investment professionals and their clients focus on their portfolios' pretax performance, and frequently ignore the almost certain likelihood that after-tax performance may differ substantially.

The source of tax value is straightforward: deferring payment of capital gains taxes. A simple example of this is a buy-and-hold investment portfolio, in which no capital gains are realized throughout the investment horizon. In essence, the buy-and-hold strategy amounts to an interest-free loan from the IRS, when compared to a strategy in which all capital gains are realized periodically. The size of that loan equals the deferred capital gains taxes for that period (for example, one year). Although capital gains taxes eventually must be paid when the portfolio is liquidated, postponing payment lets the portfolio earn additional returns that otherwise would be foregone had they been paid immediately.

A buy-and-hold strategy is an excellent passive tax management strategy, because it realizes zero capital gains during any investment period prior to liquidation. But other methods have the potential to generate even more tax savings. For example, an active tax management strategy built on tax loss harvesting also can be used. If the performance of this strategy equals that of the passive index, then realized capital losses can offset capital gains realized elsewhere in a client's portfolio. Although this strategy is not a cash inflow into the portfolio, it effectively reduces cash outflow equal to the capital gains tax that would have been paid to the IRS had those capital gains been realized. Note the tax loss harvesting strategy only *defers* the capital gains taxes; it does not avoid them. Realizing capital losses through active tax management usually results in a lower tax basis for the stocks in the portfolio, and a lower basis generally implies higher capital gains taxes once stocks are liquidated. Deferring taxes makes more dollars available in the portfolio to earn a return.

To quantify the external tax alpha and the internal tax alpha, we conducted the following numerical experiment. We built a portfolio that tracked the Russell 1000 index from January 1995 through December 2014, using daily closing price and weight information on each stock in the index throughout this period. We used the first

36 months of data to estimate the four-factor model, so the portfolio start date is December 31, 1997. We limited our tracking portfolio to 100 stocks, and its annualized tracking error was no more than 150 basis points. We assumed the tracking portfolio was rebalanced at the end of each month. To simplify the tax optimization objective, we further assumed that all realized capital gains were taxed as long term, since allowing for short-term capital gains would only increase the tax benefit. We also assumed a 20 percent long-term capital gains rate, which applies to the highest tax bracket. The average external tax alpha from January 1995 through December of 2014 was about 60 basis points per year and the average internal tax alpha was approximately 40 basis points annually.

 ## THE CONSUMER PERSPECTIVE

This chapter might be a difficult read for some consumers and even some advisors. It exposes how hard it is for a consumer to understand what is going on in their relationship with an advisor. Whether it is necessary to understand all of the figures in this chapter isn't a relevant question. The content of this chapter will be simplified for consumer consumption throughout the remainder of the book, but it's important that advisors understand what it provides. One strength of the Capital Sigma research from the consumer perspective is it clearly shows there are five key pillars where a consumer should expect value to be delivered by an advisory relationship. The next chapter takes this framework and helps advisors build value propositions around these outcomes in a way consumers can understand them.

There are a few more important points from the consumer angle in this chapter. Although few financial experts question the value of asset allocation and rebalancing, investors should remember that these strategies do not guarantee investment success. Many advisors include a disclosure like this one in their marketing materials:

Asset allocation and diversification do not assure or guarantee better performance and cannot eliminate the risk of investment losses.

Nevertheless, investors should utilize a rebalancing strategy on their own or with the help of a financial advisor. The rebalancing component is one most often missed by consumers. It doesn't seem intuitive to a noninvesting professional that you would sell what consumers think are "winning" securities only to take those proceeds and buy "losing" securities.

Advisors, traditional and robo, will use the term *portfolio optimization* to market their value proposition. Portfolio optimization is the process of selecting the percentage of various assets within a portfolio in order to deliver higher expected investment returns for each asset class. Although advisors will tout their portfolio optimization skills and strategies, it does not mean that they hold the magic formula to make this goal a reality.

Additional Areas of Advice

There were two key areas that were included in an ancillary way in planning and coaching, which are extremely important to better consumer outcomes. A financial advisor also adds value if the client needs assistance in the insurance area. The complex insurance market has many types of products to meet different needs. Each carries distinctive features and varying fee structures. The advisor weighs the client's insurance needs in the context of his entire financial picture, and recommends appropriate solutions. The financial advisor then develops an insurance plan, which must be periodically reviewed and analyzed. Selecting the right insurance plan protects clients from being overinsured or underinsured.

The last piece involves what is likely a consumer's biggest asset: his or her business. Advisors can certainly add value if they possess the tools needed to give advice to small businesses. There are going to be more and more entrepreneurs, not just the ones you see on *Shark Tank* each week. They will need advisors who can give them a wide range of advice on the many financial issues faced by businesses, such as guidance on establishing employer-sponsored retirement accounts and taxes. An advisor can help entrepreneurs with business-related and personal financial issues.

KEY TAKEAWAYS

- Understanding the value that can be created in the advisor-client relationship is a key starting point in building an advisory firm or understanding the advisor selection process. The pressures of growing regulation and completion will make defining better client outcomes a key skill for high-performing future advisors.
- There are five key areas where an advisor has the ability to provide value to end consumers: financial planning, asset class allocation and selection, investment vehicle selection, systematic

rebalancing, and tax management. We call these five areas *the pillars of value.* Consumers are likely to respond well to advisors who can use these pillars of value to show their relationship value added.

- There are ways to quantify the potential value or alpha created by the advisor in each of these five pillars of value. See Figure 4.2 for a summary of potential values by category.

- The most important pillar, financial planning, can be difficult to quantify. We believe the foundation of planning followed up by day-in and day-out coaching, removing the emotion of money, does have a quantifiable value.

- The Capital Sigma research and framework provides a way for advisors to speak to their end clients about the areas where the work they do actually does translate into better client outcomes.

CHAPTER **5**

Communicating
the *Essential*

*The single biggest problem in communication is the
illusion that it has taken place.*

—George Bernard Shaw

There's nothing worse as a consumer than being hit by a case of *cocktail party benchmarking.* "What's that?" you may ask. You are at a fiftieth birthday party for a business associate. Another guest comes up to you and starts small talk. In the course of the conversation, because it's January, the person asks, "So, how'd you do in the market last year? My advisor got me 12 percent. How did yours do for you?" Regardless of whether this conversation seems too personal or just plain nosy, many people might also feel uncertain about their financial portfolios. If their advisors returned less than 12 percent, they're likely to feel like they missed out on something. Humans are wired to be competitive, and many consumer investors feel anxious about their financial choices, making it easy for them to miss the other key variables of comparing performance: risk profile, time horizon, cash flow goals, and so on. Cocktail party benchmarking may be even worse for financial advisors when the next financial review comes around and clients demand to know why their portfolios aren't performing as well as others'. This simple example shows how many advisor-client relationships have worked in the past. As Ric Edelman puts it, "As an industry, many advisors have always had their value propositions come down to, 'I can do it cheaper,' or 'I can get you better performance.'"

In addition to raising questions about performance, cocktail party benchmarking can also lead to doubts about investment vehicles and the perceived status of being affiliated with certain companies. As Chip Roame describes, "The only real reason people seem to invest in hedge funds anymore is because they like to talk about it at parties." On the surface, the issue of cocktail party benchmarking seems silly but, it actually reveals some key opportunities in the client-advisory relationship. Here's what we can learn:

- Dissatisfaction occurs when clients don't understand or appreciate how their objectives tie to their expected and actual investment returns.

- Consumers prioritize performance too heavily. While some advisors do make performance their number one objective, most advisors, especially those with an eye to future, would not consider performance to be the only criterion of success.

- Most advisors and clients never have a discussion about how to value their relationship, so *performance becomes the consumer's only measure, by default.*

Cocktail party benchmarking isn't going away, so we want future advisors and investors to embrace it, despite the negative impact it can have on their relationships. By taking advantage of the questions raised in consumers' minds, advisors can answer questions and educate their clients about how their portfolios serve their personal needs. Imagine how different consumers' responses might be if they had deep relationships with their advisors, built on a clear understanding of their financial objectives.

ESSENTIAL ADVISOR PRINCIPLE NO. 1

The Essential Advisor clearly identifies his or her expertise and works with investors whose needs are closely aligned.

Build It Before You Can Say It

When we interviewed Mark Tibergien, CEO of Pershing Advisor Solutions, he suggested we look at one of his articles from ThinkAdvisor.com. He discusses a story about a financial advisor who drops the ball when given the opportunity to convey his message to a prospect:

> Recently, I attended a dinner where I was seated near a husband and wife who had accumulated a fair degree of wealth but had no real knowledge of how to manage its complexity. They expressed to me their desire to hire a professional. Also sitting at our table was an advisor whom I knew to be competent. I teed him up for the conversation. "John," I said, "you work with a lot of people who are good savers and are interested in hiring someone to help them manage their financial lives. How would you explain your approach to Bob and Gloria?"
>
> What followed was the most unintelligible response I have heard in a long time. John drifted into industry jargon, insulted other advisors for doing things differently and failed to look directly at the couple as he answered my question. Their grimace told me he blew it.[1]

Tibergien's story displays a fundamental mistake we see quite often. Some readers will immediately focus on the point that the advisor had no idea how to articulate his value proposition. In most cases, advisors spend far more time talking about it than building it. Advisors across the country invest in events like client appreciation dinners, barbecues, movie nights, golf tournaments, luncheons, trips to the shooting range, and paper-shredding events. Some advisors hold monthly educational dinners or lunches. These kinds of events provide a tremendous opportunity for advisors to interact with clients and prospects in a social setting. They also give prospects a chance to interact with current clients

(Continued)

---

[1] Mark Tibergien, "Wealth Is Not a Niche," ThinkAdvisor.com, November 30, 2015, www.thinkadvisor.com/author/mark-tibergien.

(*Continued*)

and hear about all the good things an advisor or firm does for them. This type of praise can be invaluable, but only if an advisor can also clearly articulate his unique value proposition, unlike the one in Tibergien's example. Not only did he botch the delivery, he also botched the planning. A value proposition requires careful thought and planning— and it needs to be solid before you describe it in a pitch. You can't move into a house before the blueprints have been drafted. In the advisory world, you can't entice new clients if your value proposition is not firmly established. Despite this fact, advisors try to all the time, often spending a lot of money to pitch something without a plan in place.

THE INDUSTRY VALUE CYCLE

One of the most interesting personalities in the sports world is Mike Krzyzewski, head men's basketball coach at Duke University and coach and chief executive of the USA Men's National Basketball Team. His long-term success is staggering, especially considering that the age difference between him and his players increases every season. We were lucky to spend some time with him last year and one of our questions for him was, "How do you continue to relate to the players now that you are recruiting and coaching athletes young enough to be your grandchildren?" He talked about the importance of "staying relevant." This meant he needed to keep up with social media to communicate with his players the way they felt comfortable. He couldn't lead if his players didn't think he understood the lives they were living. Krzyzewski believes successful people understand that they have to react to changes sparked by both external and internal forces. Advisors are in the same position. Without changing your methods to keep up with the times, you are unlikely to succeed in the long term. It's easy to run a company and spend a lot of time doing what you need to do: sell new business, take care of clients, take care of employees, and so on. A narrow focus on these fundamentals makes it easy to forget that what you do is only part of the equation. Your firm's value is also impacted by forces outside of the industry. Figure 5.1 depicts our vision of the industry value chain, what some would call the cycle of commoditization.

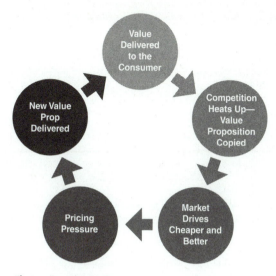

Figure 5.1 The Cycle of Value

If industry professionals and consumers were in a coffeehouse or bar enjoying one another's company, there would be differing opinions on where in the cycle the advisory industry is today. We believe we are in the stage where the market is driving cheaper options. Remember, this does not mean cheaper options *are* actually better. It means consumers perceive them to offer a better value or be at least as good as those with a higher price tag. If our placement of the investment advisory industry is correct, many firms will be forced to establish a new value proposition as the cycle proceeds to the next phase, pricing pressure.

DEFINE YOUR VALUE PROPOSITION

We spend a lot of time with advisors and leaders of firms and home offices. Usually, our role is to help a firm think about what it does and how it operates. When sitting down with a new firm or advisor, we ask some key questions:

- What do you think makes your firm unique or different?
- What would your most satisfied clients say about you?

■ What do you think is your biggest value proposition to a prospect?

We are probing to learn what the firm leadership or advisor thinks is their unique value, which should be at the center of their *value proposition*. A strong value proposition is crucial for firms as they adapt to changes in the industry and in consumer behavior. A value proposition statement should highlight their strengths and distinguishing characteristics, and how those support clients' goals. Most likely, this will focus on offerings or services that help a firm or advisor stand out from the competition.

When we ask advisors or firm leaders questions about their value proposition, one of the most common answers we get is something along the lines of, "We build customized, low-cost portfolios for our clients." That's their complete value proposition statement. They rarely mention how they do this or what distinguishing features give them an edge on the competition. To bring the problem with this into focus, we often point out that their value proposition sounds a lot like Vanguard's, with one big difference: Vanguard charges less than 50 basis points while their firm charges 100. That's usually followed by an awkward pause.

Our direct approach isn't meant to be disrespectful. It's important that advisors and leadership understand that their value proposition isn't going to work for the long term. The low costs offered by Vanguard, Schwab, and others have made it impossible for other firms to compete on price alone. This is especially true for smaller firms who can't rely on economies of scale. In all fairness, these firms are following the cycle of value, doing what they think the market wants. Looking back to Figure 5.1, you can see that as competition increases, value propositions are copied. For example, as more firms copy Vanguard's value proposition, the pool of advisors offering the exact same thing increases. This makes it even harder for them to entice new clients and compete. As a result, price becomes the primary distinguishing factor—and in the financial advisory industry, Vanguard and its peers are best positioned to win. The only way for others to gain ground is to advance to the next phase in the cycle of value and define a new value proposition.

In the industry today, there tend to be three categories of advisors:

1. Those who are not worried about their value proposition but should be.

2. Those who are not worried about their value proposition and shouldn't be.

3. Those who are worried and are actively positioning themselves for the future.

Our goal when meeting with advisors, firm leaders, and home offices is to get them into the third category.

Advisors Who Don't Worry, but Should

A value proposition that puts investment management at the center and relies on a plain vanilla thesis isn't going to work longer term. From a consumer perspective, this is a philosophy that doesn't provide a unique value. After all, every financial advisor should focus on investment management—that's a given. What consumers look for is a value proposition that is driven by asset allocation, class selection, or investment vehicle selection. Developing this type of approach takes planning, strategic thinking, and time, but it's necessary for long-term success.

Advisors Who Don't Worry and Shouldn't

The advisors who do not need to worry about their value propositions today or into the future tend to have three things in common:

1. **Put Me In, Coach:** They successfully articulate how and why they are their clients' go-to financial resource. Some firms begin that conversation by talking about investments, while others talk about planning. The starting point appears to be irrelevant. In the end, firms that don't need to worry about their own future relevance have one thing in common. They end up being number one on the client's speed dial when issues arise. As a very smart person told me years ago, "I have a wedding rule. If you are an advisor, whether that's someone's CPA, financial advisor, or lawyer, if their daughter gets married and you aren't invited to the wedding, you haven't done your job."

2. **People, People, People:** This business is about people, and the best people are only going to be more important, as spending time with clients and building relationships becomes an even greater piece of the value proposition. The best firms understand this and are investing heavily in fostering strong, long-term relationships with existing clients and prospects.

With the right value proposition, people beat robots—in terms of both financial performance and the cycle of value. But a bad value proposition or the wrong people make it pretty hard to compete with robo advisors.

3. **Succession:** This applies to advisors or firm owners older than 55. That's the age when a succession plan needs to be in place. Planning sooner can be better.

Advisors Who Worry and Work to Change

Honestly, there aren't as many advisors in this category as we would expect and, frankly, there should be more working to change. Advisors in this category understand that their value propositions are stale. Historically, most of them have placed basic investment management at the center of their philosophies, but they do not include much depth regarding product selection, class, or allocation. Firms that are ready to change realize their philosophies or methodologies overlap too much with the value propositions of digital platforms. Advisors reading this book should take a moment to determine which of the three categories they fall into. If you need some guidance, the rest of this chapter will help you figure out where your advisory firm is now and if it needs to change.

Joe Duran, CEO of United Capital, believes many advisors overlook the need to change their value propositions because they don't interact with many prospects, and instead continue on the same old methods they've been using for years with their existing clients. Most of these practices have stagnated in terms of philosophy and growth. "The people out shopping for financial advice are asking tougher questions about value and pricing. People think it's just the Millennials. It's not. It's anyone under 50," he said. "If advisors aren't growing their practices, they aren't seeing enough new purchasers. They assume their clients aren't leaving because they are satisfied with the value they are receiving. Many advisors are also missing the fact that their current clients are likely shopping more than they think. They aren't aware some of their clients are cheating on them."

Joe's comments are insightful, not only because he explains the importance of new prospects, but because he also addresses the importance of reinforcing value for current clients in addition to new ones. Talking to new prospects isn't about pitching to new clients at a country club, it's about reinforcing what you as an advisor offer, and what a consumer believes you can deliver.

You might be wondering how to assess what you should build for the future. Think back to the cocktail party benchmarking in the beginning of this chapter. With a clear and strong value proposition, the listener won't feel anxious about returns and plan to lecture his or her advisor at their next meeting. Instead, the consumer replies, "I feel fine about the return my advisor delivered for me, but that's not the only thing that matters. My advisor has helped me get very clear about my goals and is helping me ensure I reach them. That's what I think is the most important thing. I sleep well at night." Now that's a statement of confidence and value! That consumer could articulate what he or she expected from the advisory relationship—and that should be at the center of the advisor's value proposition statement. Strong relationships are built on clear expectations.

In Chapter 4 we described the five pillars of value. We intentionally use the word "pillars" because we believe these five areas provide essential support to the value proposition. An advisor should consider all of them when building a foundation for their value proposition and, more importantly, when articulating it to clients and prospects. Figure 5.2 illustrates how the five pillars form a foundation.

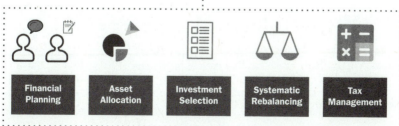

Value Proposition

| Financial Planning | Asset Allocation | Investment Selection | Systematic Rebalancing | Tax Management |

Figure 5.2 The Foundation of a Value Proposition

ASSESSING YOUR CURRENT VALUE STATEMENT

The top growth advisors and firms of the future will deliver on all five pillars of value to help end consumers reach their goals. Advisors who need to change to meet the future demands of the industry need to first answer the question: "Am I planning-focused or investment-management–focused today?" The answer has a distinct impact on the advisor-client experience and a firm's value proposition.

Remember, we use the term Capital Sigma to describe all five pillars that create the sum total of advisor-created value. Investment-focused firms build their value propositions by outperforming the benchmark and managing money. They invest around the money management pillars that are based on our Capital Sigma research: asset allocation, investment vehicle selection, and rebalancing. Planning-focused firms tend to build their value propositions around the planning-centric pillars of client value: financial planning (including coaching) and tax management. This chapter will described some of the ways investment-focused firms can differentiate and re-center their value propositions. Chapter 6 will cover the ways planning-focused firms can differentiate.

In the future, successful firms will need to deliver on all five key pillars of value. It's likely firms will still slant toward planning or investing, but they will take a comprehensive approach. Whether investment-focused or planning-focused firms are better is still up for debate. Even very smart, accomplished people have differing points of view:

- **Valerie Newell**, chairman and cofounder of Riverpoint Capital Management, argues firms will always need to be investment focused first. "It can't be all we do as a firm, but it's the most important thing we do. If the money isn't invested well, what's the point of having a good financial plan or anything else?" she asked. "People generally don't call us and say they want a financial plan. They call us and say they don't want to manage their money anymore."

- **Joe Duran:** "People aren't going to pay a lot for money management in the future. People are getting too smart," he said. "They are starting to calculate fees in dollars and not basis points and they aren't going to pay tens of thousands of dollars for something they can get with technology. Financial life management, not money management, is the future."

- ■ **Mark Tibergien**: "The industry needs to be careful making the assumption that all firms are going to build their value on financial planning. It's like everyone betting on the favorite in a sporting event," he said. "As soon as everyone seems convinced something is absolute, the other outcome occurs. As an industry, we leave ourselves exposed if we assume there won't be a way for firms to focus on money management as a value proposition in the future."

- ■ **Ric Edelman**: "You aren't going to be able to build a value proposition in the future on the value of investing," he said. "It's too difficult to outperform over the long term, impossible with passive strategies, and you aren't going to be able to make the fee argument because you aren't going to do it cheaper than the robo advisors."

There will always be firms that put investments at the center of the value equation, and we think that's fine, as long as they consider a number of key factors. The first consideration is the client mix they choose. Investment-focused firms will be challenged if they target mass-affluent or middle-market investors. These clients have less than $1 million in assets and make up about 90 percent of the overall U.S. market. Digital providers have made passive strategies and exchange-traded funds (ETFs) so easy to understand, it is difficult for advisors to add much value through portfolio management.

Recently, we visited a firm that struggled with putting investment management at the center of its philosophy. It had built its value proposition around investment management and its ability to pick individual stocks. What was most interesting was that they served clients who had portfolios of less than $1 million. The firm soon learned that it couldn't even use its own strategies because implementation was too costly. Instead, it was forced to begin adding ETFs to client portfolios. The result was a firm with a high-end value proposition but a very low-end, robo-like delivery. The lesson: *Firms with investment management at the center, without a unique angle or a unique implementation strategy, will need to serve higher-net-worth clients.*

Looking at the rebalancing pillar reveals another pitfall of an investment-managed approach. Ninety-nine percent of advisors provide no value to the end consumer if they don't use rebalancing technology. To claim otherwise is to make one of the most ridiculous arguments in the industry. Unless you are handling small-cap equity portfolios, derivatives, or a small number of fixed-income arbitrage strategies, trading is a complete waste of an advisor's time. This is one area where technology is a benefit. It frees up an advisor's time, which can be used instead on areas where an advisor makes a direct impact.

The final key consideration is differentiation. Every investment-focused firm in America believes its value proposition is unique. Despite this, these "unique" strategies are all built around momentum, macro trends, growth at a reasonable price, or some other basic principle of investment management. Some of the stories we hear are unique, but most of them aren't. For firms putting investment management at the center, there are three opportunities for differentiation: impact investing, tax-focused investing, and private investments or alternative asset classes. Often, these three critical areas are underutilized.

Impact Investing

Impact investing isn't a new concept, but people have referred to it by different names over its history. Impact investing has its roots in the days of ESG (environmental, social, and governance), a model created to assess investments based on a company's impact on those three key areas. This evolved into *socially responsible investing*, which offered a more flexible approach based on the same principles. Both iterations of impact investing were implemented based on exclusion rather than inclusion. In other words, investment strategies were a filter for what clients *didn't* want to invest in, as opposed to what best supported their investment strategy. A common example of what impact investing meant in the past is avoiding tobacco or gun companies.

Since its earliest days, impact investing has evolved to work from an inclusive perspective, whereby clients no longer create a list of things to avoid, but rather invest in companies that have a positive impact aligned with their personal preferences. Patricia Farrar-Rivas, CEO of Veris Wealth Partners, founded one of the most interesting firms in this area. She talked to us about how they build a value proposition around impact investing: "We want our clients' portfolios to be a reflection of who they are and what they care about. Studies have shown they don't have to trade performance for impact, so why not let them not only feel good about their investments helping them reach their goals, but also have a positive influence on society?" she said. Impact investing allows advisors focused on investment management the opportunity to build portfolios, not only of generic investments, but also of investments that can be customized and personalized to the individual consumer's experience.

According to the Forum for Sustainable and Responsible Investing, 69 percent of millennials believe investment decisions are a way to express their social, political, and environmental views. Based on current client research, the demand for advisors who focus on impact investing is only going to grow. Recently, at an industry event, someone challenged this claim by asking if it were possible that the research revealed a sampling bias. "If you went back in time and surveyed the Baby Boomers when they were 25 years old, wouldn't they also say they cared about social impact?" he asked. "Everyone wants to help the world when they don't have money." For an answer, we turned to Farrar-Rivas, an expert on impact investing. We asked her if she believes the interest in impact investing is declining, increasing, or staying the same. "The client demand for impact investing is only going to grow," she replied. "Just look at the investments of large institutions to validate that claim. The largest institutional advice providers are investing in entire impact-investing research departments. The profile of the consumer is also rapidly changing. We used to talk to a large percentage of the population who had no idea what impact investing was; that number is now much lower." Impact investing is one good example of how investment-focused advisors can differentiate their offerings by personalizing investment vehicles to the needs and desires of each client.

Tax-Focused Investing

It's hard to believe a future where taxes stay the same, and it's unlikely that for many advisory clients those tax rates will go down. An advisor who is investment-management centered is unlikely to be performing tax planning or tax compliance work for a client. One of the five pillars, tax management is an area where an advisor can differentiate and build value in the client relationship. Adding tax-aware investment vehicles gives the investment-centered advisor the ability to bring a third pillar of Capital Sigma into the value proposition. There are investment vehicles that allow the consumer to obtain passive, lower-cost, index-like returns, while also owning the underlying securities, unlike in index investing. This ownership of the securities gives the consumer the ability to harvest tax losses during market volatility to add tax alpha to the portfolio. At Envestnet, we call these *Quantitative Portfolios*.

Private Investments and Alternative Asset Classes

This area of investment-management differentiation is reserved for only those advisors serving high-net-worth clients because investing in many of these solutions requires accredited investor status. Some of the fastest growing firms in the country focusing on high-net-worth clients have built their value propositions on gaining access to higher risk levels through illiquid investments that also potentially deliver higher returns. The firms that do this well focus on creating additional liquidity for direct investments. Many firms will pool clients together to invest in a private equity or venture funds. Together clients can meet initial investment requirements and also have enough capital free to invest directly in the fund's offerings. (We'll walk through an example in just a moment.) These direct investments generally have a much higher return profile and, given the fund's capacity for increased due diligence, it's a little bit like getting a second bite of the apple.

For example, imagine a firm is working with a client who has a goal of putting $2 million into the private equity space. The stated minimum of the private equity fund they are looking at is $2 million. If the investor went into the fund individually, the initial investment would use the entire capital allotment. Instead, the firm pools a group of clients together and negotiates with the fund to lower minimums to $500,000 per investor. This investor now has $1.5 million available to invest. The private equity fund has a company in their portfolio looking for a $2 million investment for growth. The private equity fund has been working with this company for a long time and has a lot of confidence in the company's management, so it puts some of its own capital into the company. Then, the fund offers its investors the opportunity to coinvest with them in the company. Because the client had a lower minimum to get into the fund, he or she now has the ability to add more dollars to private equity exposure through this direct investment opportunity.

YOUR VALUE PROPOSITION: HOW TO GET STARTED

Building a value proposition seems tough. It's something consultants and industry experts tend to pontificate about it, which only makes it seem more arduous. But when you break it down into simple steps, it seems more manageable. There are two different ways to approach this task. In the first, you start with your firm. Determine what you do extremely well. Chances are, these will be they same things you and your people love to do. Then, ask three tough questions:

1. Am I better at these things than my competition?
2. How and why can I get a consumer to understand this?
3. Will the consumer be willing to pay for it now and also in the future?

If you can positively answer these questions, build the value proposition on those strengths.

Often, you can determine your strengths by defining your passion. Advisors working from this angle can begin by asking, "What am I passionate about helping clients do?" Your passion typically aligns with your strengths. For example, some advisors absolutely hate talking about Social Security and health-care planning. They don't have a competency in it, either, but they shouldn't feel they have to apologize for that. Instead, they should own it. In this example, an advisor who isn't interested in Social Security and health-care planning shouldn't target clients who are retired or in the end of the preretirement stage. Instead, they should explore their passions and see how they align with younger clients, high-net-worth individuals, or investors with specific financial interests. This may be a focus on impact investing, business planning for small business owners, or extensive depth in helping clients that like to invest in real estate. Discovering your strengths can help you define your value proposition and the investors you are best equipped to serve.

Some firms and advisors, especially given the industry's rapid change, decide to start from the client end of the equation and work from there to determine their strengths. These conversations begin by learning more about the types of clients these advisors want to serve. They segment the needs of those client profiles and build a value proposition based on their strengths and the needs of the target market. Before taking this route, it's key to understand there are a number of ways to segment clients including age, gender, geographic location, specialty needs, accumulation type (e.g., small business owner, corporate executive), client professional specialty (dentists, attorneys, farmers), and so on. Figure 5.3 illustrates a few examples of how firms select client segments to build a value proposition around.

There's a great debate about the value proposition of the future, and it's fun to hear and evaluate all the different perspectives. The debate centers on whether or not client specialization or client generalization will be the right route. Michael Kitces points out: "Many advisors are generalists. Because of this, it becomes more difficult for them to explain what they do. Unlike physicians who have specialties that involve a particular part of the body, financial planners

Client Target	Corporate Executives	Small Business Owners	Younger Clients	Retired Clients
Planning Value	· Stock option planning · Charitable planning · Retirement planning · Company benifit planning	· Defined-benefit plan design · After-sale tax transition planning · Life planning for after sale	· College funding · Maximizing company benefits · Savings/budgeting	· Social security planning · Medicare planning · Health care planning · Tax planning—maximum tax brackets
Investment Value	· Concentrated positions · Tax-sensitive vehicles	· Risk mitigation strategies	· Asset allocation · Simple investment vehicle selection · Impact investing	· Income generation · Risk mitigation · Impact investing
Other Services	· Lending	· Business consulting	· Client education	· Life planning

Figure 5.3 Customer segmentation and service delivery

have done nothing to self-organize themselves. They do not have terminology to explain what they do." Bill Schiffman, an advisor who jokes that he has more designations than sense, believes just the opposite. "As we go forward, clients need a wide variety of services," he said. "By specializing, I firmly believe advisors are giving up revenue streams available to them by providing a wide variety of services to a wide variety of clients: tax planning, wealth management, insurance, et cetera." The answer, of course, is that there is no definitive answer. Just as in Kitces's analogy of the physician, there will always be family practitioners with a wide skill set, referring tougher cases to specialists. Despite this, as the authors of this book, we owe you an opinion. Forced to choose, we come down on the side of the specialist approach. Longer-term, larger organizations will continue to create general wealth-management programs that cater to the middle-market client. It takes scale to affordably service that market, which is why the size of firms will matter even more in the future. Like in the law industry, larger firms will be able to meet the needs of a large investor base and also have deep specialized experience. As investors' net worth rises, they will begin looking for customized advice, delivered by specialists who understand their complex needs.

Don't be confused by this debate about specialization when you are creating a value proposition for your own firm. Keep things simple. Offer value by delighting the clients you want to serve. Don't try to be everything to everybody. It's a mistake many firms make and it only ends with frustrated clients and an inconsistent service model. If the value proposition you come up with centers on providing exceptional service to anyone who can pay for it, please go back to the drawing board.

HOW TO ARTICULATE YOUR VALUE PROPOSITION

Once you have established your advisory strengths and your target client demographic, it is time to move to the second step in the process, articulating your value proposition. The best value statements, regardless of theme or topic, combine four elements into a single statement.

The Elements of Winning Value Statements

1. **Attributes**, which are the fundamental characteristics of an advisor or his practice, such as size or years of experience

2. **Benefits** gained by working with the advisor

3. **Reason,** which is a rational explanation of how the firm's attributes benefit the client

4. **Emotion,** language that evokes feeling

The rest of this chapter will help you put your value proposition into words and avoid the pitfalls you might encounter along the way.

Choose the Right Words

Many advisors find it difficult to define their approaches and philosophies in plain English. When we meet with advisors and firm leaders, we tell them that if they cannot explain what sets them apart in a way that we as industry experts can understand, prospects outside the industry are not going to know what they mean at all. One of the biggest challenges here is using language that is clear while avoiding overused clichés. This balancing act is important because the statements that resonate most with consumers are easy to understand but also distinguish themselves from those of competitors.

Advisors sometimes rely on tired adjectives like *unique* to describe their firm's services. While being unique is certainly a worthy goal, it is a very hard promise to deliver on. Every firm we meet with claims to be unique, but few have the ability to elaborate on what makes them different from every other "unique" firm on the planet. There is a big difference between using a word as a label and actually providing *unique* value.

We have come across advisors using more esoteric language, like the phrase *black swan*, in their marketing materials. This isn't a term many of investors are familiar with in a financial context (although some may have seen the movie *Black Swan*, starring Natalie Portman and Mila Kunis as ballerinas). In the investment world, black swan events are random and unexpected occurrences that can be hazardous to investors. If advisors decide to use this type of jargon in materials for consumers, they need to be careful. It is important to not only define these terms for consumer investors, but also to tie the underlying concepts to your value proposition.

What Your Competitors Are Saying

We have read many studies about communicating value propositions. One of the best was conducted by Pershing and BNY Mellon.[2] After scrutinizing a number of industry value propositions, they determined that the most effective ones quickly tell investors what the advisor offers and why he or she is good to work with. The study also made the following points:

- Sixty percent of investors say all advisors make the same promises.
- Some value propositions discuss issues that investors don't really care about. (The study pointed to simplicity as one of these topics. We disagree that simplicity is unimportant and we will explore this more later in this chapter.)
- There is not enough focus on two topics that investors do care about: conservative investment approaches and trust.

  Pershing and BNY Mellon also found that when advisors address client benefits on their websites, the most commonly used phrases include:
- Meet your needs
- Meet your financial goals
- Peace of mind/simplify your life
- Build long-term relationships
- Minimize risk/maximize returns/limit tax
- Estate planning/investment management
- High-quality service

Finally, the most commonly used value theme is *developing solutions that meet the client's needs*. The most frequently mentioned attribute is independence.

---

[2] Pershing and BNY Mellon, "What Do Top Advisors Say and What Do Investors Really Think?" 2014, www.pershing.com/our-thinking/thought-leadership/what-do-top-advisors-say-and-what-do-investors-really-think.

Barry Glassman of Glassman Wealth Services has opined that financial advisors communicate the wrong messages on their websites. According to an *InvestmentNews* article, Glassman believes financial advisors need to retool their messages:

> Advisers tend to take one of two approaches on their websites: bragging about how transparent and great they are, or projecting themselves as experts in the markets or economy.
>
> The verbiage on adviser sites today nearly always includes one or more of the words fiduciary, holistic, objective or best interest, among a few others.
>
> We're not standing out to the general public by using these kinds of terms. We are using a lot of that same old, same old, which used to be special.
>
> Instead, every RIA's message should be individual, authentic, and focused on how they resonate with clients.[3]

As we discussed in Chapter 2, it is no wonder consumers think we all sound the same. Advisor websites certainly give that impression.

The Fine Print

There is one thing that is too important not to mention, at least in passing. It should go without saying that your value proposition statement will be honest and accurate. When talking about their value propositions, some advisors are tempted to bend the truth about performance or the size of the book managed. Not only is this unethical and unfair to clients, but it can also get you into trouble. Statements that fudge the numbers have come under continued scrutiny from the SEC and other regulatory bodies. Advisors do not need to go full-on Bernie Madoff to be in violation; even something an advisor perceives as harmless can run afoul of the law and also have a negative impact on client expectations. Transparency and honesty are integral

---

[3] Liz Skinner, "Advisers Using the Wrong Words on Websites to Attract New Clients," *InvestmentNews*, November 11, 2015, www.investmentnews.com/article/20151111/ FREE/151119973/advisers-using-the-wrong-words-on-websites-to-attract-new-clients.

components of any value proposition. They are fundamental to establishing trust with consumers, and they also echo our earlier advice that you must be able to deliver on your value proposition—without bending the truth.

A similar problem arises when advisors tout their *conflict-free advice*, but the fine print on their disclosure brochures (Form ADV) identifies a number of actual and potential conflicts of interest. This is especially important in the registered investment advisor (RIA) model. RIAs owe a fiduciary duty to disclose material conflicts of interest and manage those that cannot be avoided so the results are in the client's favor.

Some advisors take a buckshot approach and create multiple value propositions. They assume that if they throw out 5 or 10 ways in which they add value, at least one will resonate with prospects. Occasionally, they promise far more than any advisor can deliver. We've heard stories of seminar invitations guaranteeing consumers they will never run out of money. One even stated a firm would increase clients' income without fees or risk. The same invitation promised double-digit returns and long-term care protection without ever paying a premium.

Capture What Your Clients Feel

Financial decision making is an emotional experience for consumers. The numbers on their monthly statements represent years of hard work, the promise of their children's education, a secure retirement, and other important goals that rely in large part on the advisory relationship. The best advisor-client relationships involve emotion and a personal connection built over a long period of time. This can be very difficult to put into words. In a way, the value of the relationship comes down to what clients experience emotionally. Advisors' value comes not from what they *do* for their clients, but from how they make their clients *feel*. Before you decide that sounds a little too warm and fuzzy, consider how a client's feelings are influenced by what an advisor does. If an advisor does everything needed to fulfill his or her value proposition, clients will likely feel great about their financial position, which will lead to a number of other positive emotional experiences.

The right financial advisor can make a client feel confident, empowered, and in control of his or her future. It may seem impossible to put those feelings into words, especially when finding new clients, but we believe it is possible. One firm that has really impressed us in this respect is Aspiriant, one of the nation's largest independent wealth management firms. When they rebranded their website a few years ago, they focused on the client experience, especially how their clients feel when they are in a relationship with the firm. The result is one of the best-executed examples of articulating those feelings with words. It's a very different approach—one that we consider to be truly unique. If you want to base your value proposition on emotion, visit Aspirant's website (www.aspiriant.com) to see one in action.

Practice Your Pitch

Many advisors don't have trouble explaining *what they do* in 30 seconds, but they struggle to differentiate themselves in 30 seconds. Jay recalls a frustrating experience he had when he was an RIA. "Here I was running a higher-end firm focused on corporate executives. I met someone new on the golf course and the guy asks me what I do. I tell him and he replies, 'I have a friend at Fidelity in their 401(k) business. It sounds like you two do the same thing.'" Jay was stunned. That comparison couldn't have been further from the truth. Jay remembers his reaction, "Our firm had just gone through a rebrand and had trained on positioning. I remember being so angry. I went back to the office the next morning and explained to the team that we had a lot of work to do."

On too many occasions, financial advisors stumble when they attempt to articulate their value propositions in elevator speeches. Here are a few we hear all the time:

- We offer great customer service.
- We're very client-centric.
- We beat the benchmark.
- We are very good financial planners.
- We build customized portfolios.
- We focus on keeping costs low.

These are all great points, but everyone uses them, so they are not useful point of differentiation. To help understand what an advisor should say to prospects, Mark Tibergien recommends that advisors have an answer to the question, "Why do clients come to you and why do they stay?" According to Tibergien, success depends upon how potential clients perceive a financial advisor's skills and availability.

In Tibergien's opinion, the most important tactic for gaining new clients is to position the firm clearly in the minds of clients, prospects, peers, and centers of influence. He suggests advisors answer a few key questions and consider some important facts about your message:

> When others describe you or your firm, what do they say? What would you like them to say? Do you ever ask prospects why they came to you? Do you document these responses?

> Effective marketing means that your firm is recognized for what you do and why you do it. As you build your referral network, develop clear language that represents your firm well; not a full-on spiel but a succinct description of what makes you unique or compelling or trustworthy.

> In order to create effective language, advisors must be clear on their mission.

Make a Good First Impression

As we have mentioned, many financial advisors say their value propositions center on providing great customer service. From the largest to the smallest firms, investments are being made to enhance the client experience. People are realizing it's one of the few ways to differentiate human advisors from robo advisors. Firms are hiring for positions like *director of first impressions*, and large institutions are hiring *chief client officers*.

As the world gets noisier, differentiating the human-advisor experience may actually be easier than ever. In many cases, the first impression firms provide isn't always a good one. At some firms, the "director of first impressions" is a phone tree that is difficult to navigate. Automated answering services may be off-putting to prospects and clients, especially senior investors. Some prospects are old school and view a firm without a human answering the phone as unsuccessful. Others aren't so picky, but not many people object to being greeted by a person when they call.

Recently, Jay was at a client's office and ran into one of the firm's customers. He asked what impressed the client about the firm and his exact answer was, "Well, when I walk into a meeting, Tricia has a coffee waiting for me with one creamer and two sugars. They pay attention to me as a person and to the small details." This high praise demonstrates that the firm's value proposition is about people and not investments. Consider building your value proposition on a positive first impression.

Chip Roame, managing partner of the Tiburon Consulting Group, put it this way: "Customer service isn't what people think it is." Roame said, "Great customer service is what the *client* thinks is great customer service, not what the advisor thinks it is. There is a big disconnect in this obvious statement."

Roame had high praise for Ken Fisher, one of the industry's top marketers. The reason: "Their clients love them because of their service," Roame said. "Some other firms look down on them because they only have two offices, but these advisors don't get it. Fisher's firm touches its clients in an amazing number of ways. They are proactive and follow a very methodical approach. People say it's cookie cutter, but I will tell you their client satisfaction scores are off the charts." We in the industry have ideas about what great service looks like, but consumers often have very different opinions. If you are going to build your value proposition around client service, you had better deliver in the way the client expects! In Chapter 7 we will discuss ways to better quantify client service and client satisfaction.

Don't Overplay the Fiduciary Card

Many firms mistakenly believe their value propositions are that they are fiduciaries. Although the fiduciary relationship certainly is of value to investors, it does not separate financial advisors from other firms that are also fiduciaries. It also brings the consumer into a conceptual arena they might not understand well. Being a fiduciary is not in itself a value proposition because it does not differentiate a firm from the thousands of other advisors who are also fiduciaries.

Some advisors overplay the fiduciary card. They use broad generalizations such as, "We act in clients' best interests; other firms do not." That is akin to saying, "We care about you and they don't." It is never a good idea for financial advisors to tear down their competition. In fact, we would argue that doing so does not support a value proposition because it doesn't explain to consumers what *you* will do for them.

In February 2015, President Obama directed the Department of Labor (DOL) to push forward with proposed rulemaking to require retirement advisors to abide by a fiduciary standard. On February 23, 2015, the president told the DOL to update its rules so that retirement advisors will put the best interests of their clients above their own financial interests. He articulated a very simple principle: "You want to give financial advice? You've got to put your clients' interests first." Of course, anyone who understands the regulatory process knows doing that isn't always as simple and straightforward as you might expect.

THE VALUE PROPOSITION GOES SOCIAL

Not so long ago, advisors thought all they needed to do was slap together a website and wait for clients to call. The truth is, even if a firm has a terrific value proposition, posting it on their website is not an effective marketing tool. Furthermore, it is not enough for a financial advisor to develop a value proposition, and then wait for opportunities to communicate the message to prospective clients.

Even with the right value proposition, advisors must communicate their message to the right audiences. There are plenty of statistics that support the claim that financial advisors are using social media successfully, but we don't buy them. The numbers don't correspond to our "on the road" observations. Using a LinkedIn page to find prospects doesn't count as effective social media use.

Social media has proven to be a valuable tool for some advisors. LinkedIn is still the most used social media outlet, but it is just the tip of the iceberg. Many advisors attempt to increase visibility and name recognition by using Facebook, Twitter, and various forms of social media. Getting their names out there, however, is not enough. Advisors must also be able to communicate their value propositions and tie those to their brands. This is not always an easy task.

In a different era, advisors depended upon word of mouth to attract new clients. That still very much drives the majority of the average firm's new business, but social media trends can have lasting effects on value. Consumers frequently read and post online reviews of televisions, microwaves, or the new Indian restaurant down the street. It is also becoming more common for consumers to turn to the Web to learn about and review financial services. This online feedback plays a role similar to word of mouth, but it is much more visible and far-reaching.

Online review sites such as Yelp also pose an unexpected benefit to firms contemplating their value propositions. Advisors can see exactly what clients are saying, whether it's good or bad. They can show what consumers seem to be looking for in an advisory relationship, and they also provide a client perspective that can reveal an advisor's strengths. This information can be incredibly useful as you prepare your value proposition. (Note: We're not naïve and we know that many advisors encourage their friends and relatives to post positive reviews. In some cases, the advisors even supply the content. These phony reviews are useless and damaging, and our advice does not apply to them.)

We looked at Yelp and saw a particular financial advisor had glowing reviews from a number of clients and one negative review. (Please note that we are not using real names, and the comments have been edited.)

> Evan is very pleasant and extremely professional. I believe, however, he is not a fiduciary planner and lacks sophistication as an investment planner. He invests in funds that pay him commissions, without discussing the benefits of these funds or the costs. Although this might be okay for some investors, I believe clients deserve much more than just a standard fund and a life insurance policy.

> The fees for these very basic services are very high and do not include commissions that he makes for investing IRA accounts, which are nearly 1.5 percent. Evan did not communicate with me unless I emailed or called with a question. His answers to my questions lacked depth or

direction. As with any financial advisor, you have to be extremely cautious, educate yourself, and ask the right questions. Better yet, do the basic investment and life insurance stuff on your own. You can avoid wasting your hard-earned money on unnecessary and outrageously expensive guidance.

While it was probably of little consolation to the advisor, the reviewer gave him two stars for his pleasant demeanor and because he thoroughly investigated the client's financial situation before giving advice. There is no doubt, however, that negative reviews on social media will discourage some prospects from hiring an advisor. It's part of the sales process of the future, whether advisors like it or not. Managing client expectations and your social footprint is about more than updating your LinkedIn and Twitter accounts with helpful links.

Consumers often wonder why financial advisors don't offer many direct client testimonials. RIAs are restricted in their use of social media. Whether an RIA is SEC- or state-registered, the applicable advertising rule usually prohibits the use of testimonials. Although the word *testimonial* is not defined, the SEC has interpreted it as being a statement of a client's experience with or endorsement of an investment advisor. The rule prohibits the use of testimonials, because prospective clients may mistakenly infer that all of an RIA's clients had the same positive experience. Securities regulators also believe that any financial advisor can find someone to say good things about the firm.

Consider Your Image

Long before social media, it was difficult to reach out to prospective clients. In her book *Best Practices for Financial Advisors*, Mary Rowland wrote about a Charleston, South Carolina, financial planner who utilized a shopping cart promotion. The planner, Kyra Morris, advertised her firm by plastering her face and phone number on grocery shopping carts. Although the marketing campaign brought her a lot of attention and some laughs, it did not bring her the clients she wanted to target.[4]

---

[4] Mary Rowland, *Best Practices for Financial Advisors* (Princeton, NJ: Bloomberg Press, 1997), 206–207.

Talk to the Right Audience

One key question in the communication of the value proposition is: *Who is the audience?* By the time you begin creating your value statement, you should already know what types of clients pair best with your strengths and approach. Now it's time to make sure you are talking to your target audience. This probably sounds obvious, but it's something we hadn't thought of until we talked with Ric Edelman. He cautioned that most firms are so focused on their reputation within the industry that they forget to address consumers in their value proposition. And consumers are the people who matter most. "If you aren't at a large brokerage firm, it's hard to have a brand and message get to the end consumer," Ric said. "In the industry, a lot of firms are excited to be known for one thing or the other, but if the end consumer doesn't know who you are or how to find you, it doesn't do anything for your business."

Chasing Younger Clients

It's impossible to read any financial services industry website or publication without coming across articles about Millennials. The terms *emerging investors* and *Next Gen* also refer to this demographic, specifically to people younger than age 30.

The financial services industry has wrestled with the question of whether targeting emerging investors is a promising way to build growth. *Envestnet found that the top growth advisors are paying attention to and are targeting the next generation of investors, growing assets in this age segment at a rate of 15 times the overall peer group.* The top advisors are also growing the asset base of clients in the 60-plus age demographic at 15 times the overall rate. In the other age categories, the top-quartile advisors were still growing faster, but not as noticeably as the two end categories. We dug deeper into this barbell effect and it played out as we expected: The top-growth advisors are not only winning on the top end, but they are also winning with their clients' children.

As the average age of advisors skews older, it becomes more difficult for them to figure out how to market to younger prospects. By looking for new clients in the same old places, advisors intentionally or inadvertently overlook Millennials, a group that has or will have significant assets and is thirsty for financial advice.

Recently we encountered a funny article that displays some of the problems around marketing to younger consumers. Paul Brady, a millennial, wrote an article entitled "Millennials to Hotels: Stop Trying So Hard." Brady went on a rant about how older hotel executives like Bill Marriott and Ian Schrager keep trying to attract young guests by putting record players and street art in their rooms. A new InterContinental Hotels Group brand serves kale salads and has LED mood lighting next to every bed. Brady argued that hotels don't need to sell Millennials with in-room acoustic guitars. The author was more excited by the bedside outlet where he could charge his phone while it rested on the nightstand. "It turns out we're not that different from our parents," Brady informed readers. "Just don't skimp on the free Wi-Fi."[5] At 36 years old, Jay straddles Generation X and the Millennials. "I agree with Paul Brady," he says. "I hate when people see that I'm younger and assume I play on Facebook all day, or that my first preference for picking a job is whether or not I can bring my dog to work."

Firms wishing to build for the long term can't afford to ignore the future generations of clients. The 2015 Capgemini and RBC Wealth Management World Wealth Report surveyed wealthy people in 23 countries.[6] It provides a great deal of information that advisors can use to identify their value propositions. The report found there are more high-net-worth investors than ever. High-net-worth investors are defined as individuals with more than $1 million in investable assets. In 2014, the number of high-net-worth individuals rose 8.6 percent to 4.4 million.

Young people are likely to inherit much of that wealth through future generational wealth transfer. *InvestmentNews* reported there will be a $30 trillion wealth transfer from Baby Boomers to Generation X to Millennials over the next 30 years. The transfer has already begun and it has resulted in some interesting trends so far. Once they have inherited the wealth, roughly two-thirds of children leave their parents' financial advisors—taking that money with them. An *InvestmentNews* survey found that 66 percent of children terminate their parents' financial

---

[5] Paul Brady, "Millennials to Hotels: Stop Trying So Hard!," *Condé Nast*, January 2016, 116.

[6] Capgemini and RBC Wealth Management. "World Wealth Report 2015," June 17, 2015.

advisors after inheriting their wealth.[7] This poses a huge incentive for advisors to entice young people to sign on with them. It may, however, be difficult to market to the younger generation. High-net-worth prospects who are under 40 have less trust, satisfaction, and confidence in wealth managers than the older generations of clients. Younger clients with a high net worth are less sticky, which means they are less likely to have permanent relationships with their financial advisors if they are not satisfied. This raises the question of whether advisors should connect with each generation with a different value proposition. For example, estate planning is much less of a concern for younger clients, and the value provided to older clients in this area is far greater than for a young couple with no children. The older client is far more likely to be focused on legacy wishes and charitable giving. Based on those assumptions, an advisor whose value proposition is centered on estate planning will have difficulty marketing to younger clients.

The perception is that younger consumers prefer robo advisors to human ones. In research released in May 2015, Schwab found that two-thirds of the surveyed investors preferred a human touch when it came to investing. Furthermore, Gen-Xers are just as likely as Millennials to prefer their portfolios be based on computer algorithms.[8]

According to the Capgemini U.S. Wealth Report, among wealth management clients who are under age 40, there is a phenomenal demand for digital services and automated advice platforms. Among wealth management clients who are under 30, the demand is even higher. Seventy-seven percent of clients under age 30 said they would leave a wealth manager who did not offer digital communication and service channels. Ninety percent of clients under 30 are interacting digitally, while only one-third of clients over 60 interact digitally.[9]

---

[7] Liz Skinner, "The great wealth transfer is coming, putting advisers at risk," *Investment News*, July 13, 2015, www.investmentnews.com/article/20150713/FEATURE/150719999/the-great-wealth-transfer-is-coming-putting-advisers-at-risk.

[8] "Man and Machines: New Charles Schwab Study Examines How Different Generations Approach the Use of Technology," May 12, 2015, http://pressroom.aboutschwab.com/press-release/schwab-investor-services-news/man-and-machines-new-charles-schwab-study-examines-how-d.

[9] "U.S. Wealth Report: Record Highs; Major Challenges," *Financial Planning*, December 3, 2015, www.financial-planning.com/news/industry/us-wealth-report-record-highs-major-challenges-2695023-1.html.

A study from the Spectrem Group found that younger investors in employer-sponsored retirement plans are moving away from using advisors for financial services. More than 40 percent of participants under age 35 stated they are making their own investment decisions. Roughly one-third of participants ages 35 to 49 engaged in similar behavior.[10] On the bright side, more than 30 percent of plan participants said they will be seeking advice on long-term-care planning, tax-advantaged strategies, and estate planning. This indicates that the consumers of the future will look for services that focus more on planning and less on investment management.

THE CONSUMER PERSPECTIVE

Many advisors hear the cocktail party speeches from wealth managers who talk about where to find alpha in up or down markets, but the consumer conversation is far different. It's clear investors are growing skeptical of advisors who use jargon and talk big numbers. Savvy investors ask questions like "How did those returns compare to a benchmark like the S&P 500?" Better yet, they would ask, "How well did your wealth manager do in 2008 when the bottom fell out of the market?" There wasn't a lot of cocktail party benchmarking back in 2008, because few people wanted to brag about who lost less money.

Today, at cocktail parties, the "F word" is being thrown around quite a bit. In this case, the "F word" is *fiduciary.* From a consumer's point of view, advisors are overusing this buzzword on their websites, social media postings, and in blogs. It appears they believe that being a fiduciary differentiates them from every other firm that is making the exact same pitch.

For a consumer, an advisor who draws attention to the fact that he's acting in the client's best interest is stating what should be obvious. Even worse, some consumers believe firms use the word to cover themselves when they are engaging in irresponsible behavior. After all, Bernie Madoff claimed he was a fiduciary. There's a clever analogy that a financial advisor overusing the work *fiduciary* is like going to a jeweler who constantly reminds customers that they sell *real diamonds.* It's pretty much a given that when you go to a reputable jeweler in search of a quality stone, you're going to get a real diamond. Likewise, financial consumers expect advisors to

(Continued)

---

[10] "New Spectrem Study Shows Younger Investors in Employer-Sponsored Retirement Plans Shifting Away From Advisors," Reuters, December 16, 2015, www.reuters.com/article/idUSnMKWJGdzBa+1f2+MKW20151216.

(*Continued*)

act in the client's best interest. From the consumer's vantage point, advisors should rethink their career choices if they're not going to live up to the fiduciary standard. As stated in earlier chapters, people don't trust Wall Street.

Advisors should use events and marketing materials to talk about their areas of specialization. At WealthRamp, Pam Krueger matches the consumers' financial needs with an advisor who specializes in handling those concerns, and she also includes how the investor would like to interact with an advisor. For example, a woman who has just gone through a divorce is very likely to seek out a new advisor relationship to help her sort out priorities and invest accordingly. She may want someone who will guide her through a maze of financial decisions that are brand new to her. She may tend to feel most comfortable working with a proactive advisor who has expertise in divorce settlements and is also a great communicator.

Without specialization, advisors will drown in a sea of sameness. For decades, brokerage firms have spent billions to build up their Wall Street name brands. The fact is, consumers have been trained to believe all the advisors at those highly recognized name-brand firms offer the exact same expertise. After all, when people choose a brand name, they often assume all its employees fit the brand's profile. Think about it: many ad campaigns may have actually backfired because the public has bought into the story that every advisor can do the same thing and that they all use the same approach. There are no longer individual advisors. Instead, they are an army of plain vanilla clones. Now think about the opportunity this message campaign has created for individual advisors. The first step is for advisors to look at themselves through the eyes of the consumer and ask, "What makes me that different?" Then, they should zero in on that unique offering and practice the heck out of getting that point across.

Consumers have grown tired of gimmicks and they're skeptical of advisors. They've come to realize that regulators exist as the policemen, but regulators can't necessarily protect them from advisors who give lip service to being fiduciaries but don't act accordingly. Consumers need to learn how to do their own due diligence. There are lots of free, online investor education resources where anyone can get very practical, real-world tips to protect themselves from potential financial abuses. Once individual investors learn how to recognize the biggest red flags, they can read and actually understand the disclosures provided by an advisor. As an example, when a consumer is educated, he or she will realize there's a problem if an advisor hasn't been up front about clarifying any issues in question during introductory meetings. Instead of accepting a persuasive sales pitch, a savvy investor will think, "This advisor doesn't possess the qualities I want in the person handling my most serious money decisions, even if I enjoyed our conversation over lunch."

CONCLUSION

Developing a solid value proposition is a challenging task. In addition to determining the foundation of your message—your strengths and ideal client type, you need to express it with the right language and decide how to tailor it to reach different consumer demographics. If you feel overwhelmed, remember this advice from Mark Tibergien: "This business is always going to be about people." We couldn't agree more. How do advisors build deeper relationships with clients? This is the real value, which we will explore in Chapter 6.

KEY TAKEAWAYS

- Embrace cocktail party benchmarking. See it as an opportunity for your clients to talk about what you do for them. To lay the groundwork for this kind of interaction, talk to your clients about what a successful advisory relationship looks like, and what it includes beyond investment performance. That way, they will be able to reframe cocktail party comments in a more appropriate context.

- A differentiated value proposition is important, but its success depends on its execution. Two firms might have similar statements of value, but the firm that more strongly delivers always wins.

- Firms tend to be focused on either investment management or financial planning. There will be more financial planning firms in the future as it becomes harder for firms to differentiate on the grounds of investment management.

- A firm can create their value proposition in one of two ways. It can build it around its greatest strength, or it can determine the type of client it wants to serve and work backward from the needs of that investor base.

- If you are going to build your value proposition around client service, that level of service needs to meet your customers' expectations for exceptional service. It cannot be what the firm dictates as exceptional.

CHAPTER 6

Building the Essential Relationship

Who Are You Going to Call?

Will the Internet kill your free community paper? Did instant potatoes kill potatoes?

—South Florida community newsletter

A community newspaper in South Florida asked those questions in a one-page advertisement that included a huge picture of a baked potato. The ad copy began by saying "New technologies change many things. But not everything. You may tweet, blog, surf, shop, or search online but you continue to read your free community newspaper. You just proved it." Although the Internet has not killed newspapers, they have been seriously wounded. They have had to adapt in order to survive.

THE POWER OF RELATIONSHIPS

A man in South Florida went to a walk-in medical clinic after suffering an injury to his shoulder. As he filled out his medical form, he came to the question, "What is the reason for your visit?" He joked, "The Internet was down."

In speeches, we, like others, have compared the WebMD online medical reference to the digital advice movement, but it really hits home when the analogy comes to life. Several years ago, Jay kept getting dizzy spells. He thought it might be vertigo. Jay searched the Internet first, as most of us do when a medical issue arises. That was a huge mistake. The search results returned a frightening list of dizziness causes including Parkinson's disease, brain tumors, and stroke. Full of anxiety, Jay went to see his family doctor for an actual diagnosis. Jay's doctor has known him for nearly 20 years and listened patiently. He noticed Jay's demeanor was different and asked about his level of stress. Instead of sending Jay for a battery of tests, the doctor's pre-scription was for a little less work and Diet Coke, and a little more sleep and water. If the doctor had not been able to assess Jay's behavior, comparing it to a baseline built through years of interaction, Jay probably would have ended up in an MRI machine.

Elliot Weissbluth, CEO of Hightower Advisor Partners, grew up as the son of a famous pediatric doctor who helped parents solve deep sleeping issues with their infant children. Weissbluth talked to us about what it was like to watch his father interact with patients: "Much of the time when he diagnosed a problem it wasn't by a medical exam, but it was by reading people. He could tell how bad it was based on the reaction of the parents. What he's done his whole life is read people and their emotions and I believe great financial advisors do the same thing." He argues that as investment management becomes more commoditized, financial planning is quickly becoming the next focus area of value. "It isn't the value of the financial plan, the value is in the person interpreting it with the client . . . helping them understand what the output means in their life and reading the emotional responses is the value." We call this the *intersection* of a client's financial situation and emotional situation (see Figure 6.1).

Figure 6.1 The Intersection

ESSENTIAL ADVISOR PRINCIPLE NO. 2

The Essential Advisor helps investors cut through the noise to achieve better financial and personal outcomes.

Value Is in the Intersection

In Chapter 2 we talked about the noise caused by complexity. What we did not discuss is how an advisor can spot moments where they provide maximum value and comfort to an investor, making advice absolutely *essential.* We believe investors have a number of moments throughout their lives when the financial situations they are experiencing overlap with the emotional elements of being human. Some of these items may be small and some can be life-changing events. When the financial and the emotional collide, as depicted in Figure 6.1, there tends to be an overlap or *intersection* where advice is needed. This intersection is where an advisor is needed more than ever. The advisor has the ability, through a deep understanding of the client, to understand how wide or narrow this intersection is and how the investor or his or her family can get to a resolution everyone feels good about. One simple example is the financial and emotional overlap of an investor having to make the decision of whether to keep the mortgage on his house or to pay it off when he and his wife retire.

For investors reading this: Please note this is not financial advice. In many cases the argument could be made to keep a mortgage in retirement, as it may create a tax benefit. The following example of an

(Continued)

(*Continued*)

advisor who is essential to her clients helps illustrate how this decision can be made. Chris and his wife, Molly, are both about to retire and they sit down with their advisor to discuss the issues around the retirement. As they discuss the issue of mortgage payoff, their advisor lays out the numbers and recommends keeping the mortgage due to the tax savings. As their advisor is walking them through the costs and savings, she senses Chris start to get tense. She asks Chris why he seems to be reacting negatively to the analysis. Chris doesn't really put his finger on it immediately, but his advisor has seen this before. She asks Chris if he's concerned about cash flow in retirement and he says he is. The advisor then goes on to ask him if the mortgage is going to cause him stress as he thinks about their finances in retirement. That was the issue. Chris didn't want to be lying in bed, worrying about a mortgage payment. The advisor and the couple decide the tax savings isn't worth the sleepless nights and they decide to pay off the mortgage as soon as Chris and Molly retire. Had the advisor not been able to read Chris or understand his concerns, she likely would have continued to recommend a financial option that was right on paper, but wrong in practice. Imagine if Chris and Molly were trying to make this decision working with a robo-advice platform that ignored the emotional aspects of the decision. This seems like a small and silly example, but it likely happens in hundreds of advisory firms every week.

One of the most emotional meetings we have ever attended involved an advisor and a family making a decision about college funding. This was a topic the family had been discussing for quite some time. About three years earlier, the advisor and couple had sat down and used proceeds from an equity grant to supply the remaining amounts needed to fund college for their two kids. In that meeting there was a deep discussion around the principles the parents had when it came to how they were going to pay for their two children's college education. They both had graduated from college with immense amounts of student-loan debt and they wanted their kids to avoid the same situation. However, they wanted to cap how much they would pay because they wanted to encourage a strong work ethic in their children. At the time, they determined the amount they would need based on the tuition of a reasonable state college. Now, three years later, their daughter had been accepted into NYU, one of the country's premier universities, which was also significantly more expensive than they had originally planned.

The emotional anguish of the parents was obvious. It was an exciting time but they were struggling greatly with the decision about what to do. Could they afford to help her pay more? If they did, how could they make it up to their younger son? Is it fair they pay more for her and less for him? If they tell their daughter they can't pay the entire amount for tuition and board, would she feel like they were limiting her opportunities? The questions continued and it was apparent the couple wasn't on the same page. The advisor had a lot to navigate in the meeting. He asked probing questions, challenging one parent and then the other about what the desired outcome should be. Prior to the meeting, the advisor had prepared a new financial plan so the couple could understand the tradeoffs of increased college funding and retirement funding. After two hours, the couple made a decision, their stress visibly lifted from their demeanor. They left the advisor's office no longer feeling stressed, but excited (as they should have been), as they went from being younger adults with school debt to being parents able to help their daughter to go to NYU—a dream come true. The advisor that day made a meaningful impact on that family forever.

ESSENTIAL ADVISOR PRINCIPLE NO. 3

The Essential Advisor is the first call when a client is faced with a life transition, responding with true care and concern.

The intersection moments are sometimes as simple as the mortgage calculation, but oftentimes they can be more difficult. As we referenced in the previous chapter, advisors tend to be planning- or investment-centric and they build other services around this bias. We dug deeper into opportunities for differentiation for investment-centric firms in Chapter 5. In this chapter we want to dig deeper into the

(Continued)

(*Continued*)

relationship-building aspects of becoming essential and how firms can put financial planning and life transitions at the center of a differentiated value proposition. *Consumers don't understand what financial planning is, but they clearly understand when they need to reach out for advice.* It's difficult to define financial planning and coaching, so let's use a qualifier that applies to other relationships: If you were in trouble, after you called a family member, who would be the next person you'd call? Again, not everyone wants a relationship this deep with their advisor, but we believe the advisors who will be truly essential in the future are the ones who would receive the call.

TRANSITIONS CLIENTS AND ADVISORS ENCOUNTER TOGETHER

Planning for college is just one of the intersection opportunities where advisors can make themselves essential. We analyzed the glide path of the typical client's life and have identified 11 key transitions where advice is needed. Some readers will argue there are many more and they're right; we could have likely come up with 50 transitions, but we focused on the ones where an investor or family would be most likely to need advice and where an advisor's impact would be greatest.

No. 1: First Job and Benefits Choices

If we had a dollar for every time we hear the statement "We don't know how to build a relationship with client's kids," we'd already be retired. We think focusing on this first transition is an answer to this challenge. As a parent, having a child start his or her first job is an exciting time. In most cases, adult children have just graduated from college and likely believe they know everything about the world. What's ironic is that the advisor's advice on health care or retirement savings plan options isn't going to be much different from what a parent would tell a child in an attempt to help. However, when this advice comes from a third party, the child considers it to be more intelligent than anything a parent could provide. If you are a parent and want your child to begin building a relationship with your advisor, this is a key time to begin that process. For advisors, it's a relatively simple way to begin supporting the next generation of clients. It could also be an opportunity for a more junior person in the firm to gain practical experience while delivering advice to someone in their own age demographic, while also keeping the risk relatively low to the firm.

No. 2: Marriage

Although the average age in the United States of those getting married continues to rise, a majority of people getting married are still under 30 years old. This is yet another opportunity for a client's child to get independent advice and also allow the child and advisor to begin building a relationship. Key areas of focus here are:

- How to budget for the wedding and life after the wedding.
- Take emotion out of difficult questions (e.g., shared versus non-shared checking accounts, etc.).
- Are beneficiary forms filled out properly for employment retirement plans and life insurance?
- Is life insurance needed now and into the future?

Anyone that's ever been married knows at times things can be stressful. Helping clients or their children get off to a strong financial start in marriage is a key foundation of a relationship—and a good advisor can support that effort.

No. 3: Buying a Home

This is an area where there is a distinct bifurcation in this transition depending on the type of investor you are or the type of clients you as an advisor serve. For advisors serving middle-market clients or younger clients, lending options and mortgage selections are the key value-add in this transition. This is also where some younger consumers will use digital tools and likely won't be seeking human advisor assistance on the topic.

For advisors who work with more affluent clients, a home purchase is another key part of a planning-centered value proposition.

Even wealthy, well-educated consumers need help during this transition. Oftentimes questions arise about: the benefits of paying cash instead of securing a mortgage, the wisdom or stupidity of waiving contingencies when buying a house in California, or what assets to liquidate for a down payment or payment in full. These are topics that come up rarely for consumers, but for focused advisors they should be easy areas to provide value and expertise.

First-Time Buyers (and Their Parents)

For advisors and their higher-net-worth families, and adult child's first home purchase is a key area for advisors and investors to maximize the value in their relationship. One key question during this life event centers on whether or not parents should help children with a down payment. The answer often comes down to the family's principles, including how parents and children view money or how the parents want the children to view money. This can be a highly emotional decision. On the one hand, parents can feel the urge to help, but worry that their kids might develop an unhealthy sense of entitlement. On the other hand, kids can feel like their parents aren't being helpful enough during a major step in their lives. Helping families sort through this is a valuable service.

Jonathan Clements, a well-known personal finance writer and author, offers a creative solution to parents who want to help their children buy a home. Clements discussed this solution in an article in the online edition of *On Wall Street*. One of his seven smartest financial moves, he said, was to finance a private mortgage for his 27-year-old daughter's first home. Clements gave this description of his financial strategy:

> This year, I lent my daughter $381,000 so she could buy her first home. It was a good deal for her: She was able to behave like a cash buyer when bidding on properties; she didn't have the hassle of dealing with a bank and her closing costs were far lower.

> It was also a good deal for me. We settled on the current average rate for a 30-year fixed-rate mortgage, which was 3.97 percent. That's more than I could earn by buying

high-quality bonds. To keep everything on the level, we used National Family Mortgage in Belmont, Mass., to handle the paperwork and service the loan.[1]

Clements felt this was a smart move, and not a risky one, because he had taught his children good financial habits.

It is doubtful that most parents have this kind of generosity in mind when a life event triggers them to pick up the phone to call a financial advisor. Although they may want an advisor's advice on how to help their child buy a home, not many are willing—or able—to offer this much assistance. A financial advisor can offer advice that stops far short of lending $381,000 to a child for her first home, even with a third party servicing the loan.

No. 4: Receiving Equity or Purchasing a Business

Some readers may find these transitions unfamiliar or unlikely. They are completely dependent on what consumers do for a living and on the type of clients an advisor serves. When a corporate executive receives stock options or equity in a company, he or she has immediate planning needs. It opens the door to planning around other life transitions, such as should the person exercise options to buy a house or get a mortgage instead. Stock options often provide significant upside return potential, but investors can sometimes utilize them like a savings account instead of an investment, leaving potential return on the table. For example, exercising an option to buy a car is quite common, but it might not be the best decision for the long term. Consider that taking a loan for the car costs 3 percent per year and the equity stock option may have the potential to return 10 percent or more. In deciding to cash out stock options to buy a car, the client would be spending an investment with a potential 10 percent return to avoid a 3 percent interest rate on an auto loan.

Small business owners and their advisors run into similar dilemmas. When buying a new business, one frequent question concerns the

---

[1] Jonathan Clements, "My 7 Smartest Financial Moves," *On Wall Street*, November 30, 2015, www.financial-planning.com/news/practice/my-7-smartest-financial-moves-2694967-1.html.

amount of equity owners should contribute from their own pockets versus the amount that should come from leveraging the business to meet those financial needs.

No. 5: Birth of Child

Readers may look at this transition and think, "That's an easy transition to support. Just talk about college planning." While on the surface this seems like a simple topic, this life event can lead to some unexpectedly complex questions. Aside from college planning, the birth of a child also presents more immediate needs, especially relating to childcare. If one spouse wants to stay home, can the family afford that decision? How do you handle payroll and the tax consequences of hiring a nanny?

Then, there are the more typical questions about college planning: How much should parents be saving and in what vehicles? What about grandparents who want to support their grandchildren? Should they put money into 529 plans? How do you calculate how much to save when you haven't determined principles guiding what your children will pay for college? Will you pay 100 percent, 0 percent, somewhere in between, or will you create a matching program where you pay a certain amount to match every dollar children earn while working? On the surface, these are all pretty obvious questions, but they represent the intersection of emotion and finance, so they can be difficult to make.

No. 6: Divorce

Unfortunately, not all the transitions are positive ones, but they happen nevertheless. There are certainly legal implications, but the intersection of emotion and finance during a divorce situation may require consumers to obtain outside help. Even simple things like changing beneficiaries, estate-planning documents, and so on can be difficult to focus on during a stressful divorce. Couples will likely need to consult with an advisor on how to split assets to minimize tax consequences or continue to meet charitable goals. These are just a few of the areas where financial advisors can provide value and support. Some of the top growth firms in the country have made divorce transitioning, especially for females, their key core competency.

No. 7: Aging Parents

This is only going to become a more common transition as the baby boomer generation continues to age. How should children handle the emotional and financial consequences of taking care of their parents? Should they keep their parents in their current house or move them to a facility? What are the financial implications of each situation? Caring for an aging parent is one of the hardest transitions that exist and it's an area where consumers will need continued financial and emotional advice.

No. 8: Retirement

Retirement is one of the biggest transitions many people will ever make—and it serves as the most common transition for firms to build their value proposition around. The obvious transition topics include Social Security planning and income planning. However, what we are seeing from the top firms is an investment in two things: health insurance planning and life planning. Our friends Keith Lawrence and Alan Spector interviewed hundreds of baby boomers and thousands of others for their book, *Your Retirement Quest: 10 Secrets for Creating and Living a Fulfilling Retirement.* In it, they lay out the case that many Americans are not prepared for retirement and need assistance in not only planning for retirement, but also living in retirement. They told us, "Many people have linked their personal identity to their work, and are at a great risk of failing retirement. They are unaware of the risks before them. For example, the highest suicide rate in our country today is men over the age of 70, who struggle to replace the purpose they found at work once they are no longer working. The fastest growing divorce rate is couples over the age of 55, as relationship issues are heightened now that partners are together much more." Lawrence and Spector have been traveling the country coaching advisors on building life plans with clients to help them be more prepared for retirement. Imagine the type of deep relationship that can be built on trying to map out an amazing retirement. We are thinking the discussion of performance against a benchmark would disappear in this type of relationship, bringing clients a more comfortable future.

Health-care planning is equally as important. Regardless of the changing regulations of open or closed insurance exchanges, making the correct health-care decisions is a monumental and stressful task. For retirees, health insurance costs are by far the largest nondiscretionary expense on their household income statements. What many advisors and consumers also miss is the need for continued support in the decision-making process. There are health-care variables that change annually, for example, the drugs the consumer takes or the need for home health-care support. As the variables change, reassessing the annual renewal choices becomes even more important.

No. 9: Long-Term Care Decisions

Many baby boomers currently taking care of aging parents have quickly realized they don't want to leave their children in a similar situation, bringing long-term care (LTC) issues and insurance planning to the top of the priority list. The LTC insurance market is extremely complex. Carriers occasionally enter and exit the market, and changes to policy structures and financial arrangements make it difficult for consumers to understand their options. Navigating the LTC insurance market can be a place where good advice will make a profound difference. The decisions made during this transition are based on much more than the financial calculations. Does having insurance make it more likely that someone will make the tough decision of putting a partner in an assisted living facility instead of trying to be the caregiver at home—potentially threatening the health of them both? Does LTC insurance encourage children to make better decisions about their parents' living situation? If the costs of moving them to a facility are already taken care of, children aren't faced with the choice of spending their inheritance. It's a shame to say it, but money clouds judgement. The Essential Advisor steps in during this transition and makes sure everyone is treated with dignity and respect.

No. 10: Illness or Death of a Spouse

Nobody wants to see a spouse fall gravely ill or pass away. Both situations are highly emotional, but they also require good financial decision making. When a severe diagnosis is made, the Essential Advisor will immediately work with the client's estate-planning attorney to ensure estate documents and assets are titled in the right way, so the family can be prepared when a tragic event occurs. Although firms that put financial planning at the center of their value propositions should already have completed this, it's always best to check.

LLBH Private Wealth Management dealt with a life transition involving a recently widowed client who came to the firm in the late 1990s with a portfolio comprised almost entirely of telecommunications stocks. Both the widow and her husband were employed by a telephone company, which led to their investing heavily in that particular industry. The widow had done so well with those kinds of equities, she was reluctant to diversify. LLBH worked diligently to achieve the client's optimal asset allocation through rebalancing. As a result of the portfolio's diversified asset and sector allocation, the client avoided the Internet bubble when telecommunications stocks plummeted. Handling sickness and death entails much more than just estate planning; it's about taking in the entire financial and emotional picture.

No. 11: Legacy Issues

We strongly believe legacy planning isn't just for the super wealthy. The high-net-worth clients need to think about a number of things: Is a donor-advised fund (DAF) better than setting up a foundation? Should the donor-advised fund sit at a local foundation or at a custodian like Schwab or Fidelity? Should the legacy and planning be built around other planning vehicles like charitable lead trusts or charitable remainder trusts? Other legacy issues are equally as important, regardless of a client's net worth. If they have kids, how do they talk to them about money issues? If charity and giving back to the community is important, how do they continue to use the resources they have to encourage this?

Obviously, clients will not necessarily face all of these life transitions. Furthermore, they may not need an advisor's assistance with these transitions. There is, however, one absolute: no matter how sophisticated robo advisors become, they will never get a client through these challenges without a human element.

BUILDING AROUND THE TRANSITIONS

The Essential Advisors build their practices and firms around many of these transitions. Some will choose a large number. Some will choose a few. Some will specialize around the transitions and build their value proposition on it. There are firms that specialize only in retirement planning or deep estate planning. Others will build a more generalist approach. Whether an advisor or firm specializes on any of these transitions, an operating model is needed to deliver exceptional services built around it. There are key operational considerations for an advisor to deliver outstanding advice during the transition. They are education, specialized knowledge through experience, partnership, and technology and reporting.

Education

Consumers facing a major life transition are often going through something new to them, and they may not have friends or family members who have experienced it either. Many consumers are more comfortable when they are informed, and they rely on their advisor to provide them with necessary information. Some consumers value emotional support above this type of education, but they still need to understand how the facts apply to their circumstances. In the same way a doctor focuses on limiting anxiety by getting cancer patients to understand the facts about their treatment, an advisor can do the same for a consumer going through a transition. This may happen during in-person meetings or it may come through educational materials. Consumers need to get grounded in the facts and understand the situation at hand to minimize anxiety as much as possible. When a consumer's emotional and financial experiences intersect, some anxiety is unavoidable, but education can bring clear-headedness.

Specialized Knowledge through Experience

Consumers will go through many of the transitions we laid out earlier only once in their life. If they go through some of them more than that, the number will still be small. The advisors building their value around these life events have specialized knowledge built by seeing clients deal with these events on an almost constant basis, depending on practice size. Clients benefit from an advisor's steady hand, which comes from helping many other investors in similar circumstances. Some transitions, such as the death of a spouse, require deep subject matter expertise. Advisors and firms will have to determine how they build that expertise in-house if that is a desired outcome.

Partnership

As advisors assess the specialized knowledge they want to build within the firm or practice, they also need to assess whether or not partnership with outside entities is the right strategy to bridge the gap. Partnering with the right law firm or the right accounting firm will help advisors provide the best outcomes to clients without having to invest internally, especially for things that go beyond an advisor's core competency. Shirl Penney spends a significant amount of time with some of the largest and most sophisticated independent wealth teams in the country and he believes these types of partnerships are necessary to the successful advisory model of the future: "You need to wrap yourself around the needs of the client and help them get better advice. This doesn't mean you have to go it alone, but you need to be the central focus of bringing all of the subject matter experts together."

Technology and Reporting

The only way to be able to deliver during times of transition is to have the ability to spend time with clients. Although materials can be created to help educate a consumer, it's impossible to have a document or digital tool navigate some of these challenges. The key to managing these transitions will come from integrating a technology platform that creates efficiencies and frees up valuable capacity so advisors can spend more time with clients one on one. We will dig more into how this can be built in a later chapter.

TRANSITIONS EXPOSE DIGITAL-ONLY PLATFORMS

If you think back through the transitions or the consumer life cycle, clients needing financial life advice really live their lives in three main stages:

1. **Accumulation:** The period of time when they are accumulating assets. They are working and are trying to save and invest for life goals.

2. **Deaccumulation:** The time has come for the investor to spend the money they have saved and invested. This generally occurs in retirement.

3. **Transfer:** The time has come for the investor to transfer money to loved ones and charities, and to pass other legacy items to the next generation.

If you review the 11 major transitions and other smaller transitions consumers will go through throughout their lives, they occur in each of these three categories. We believe one of the reasons the digital-only platforms have caught on with a younger generation is because they are focused on serving the consumer in the accumulation stage. As an investor moves toward the deaccumulation stage, it's hard to see how the current digital-only platforms will have the ability to adequately serve the needs of consumers in this category. As we have previously stated, income planning, Social Security planning, and health-care planning are all foundational issues for investors in the deaccumulation stage of life. It is equally difficult to see how the robo platforms even remotely serve the client need of legacy transfer. Consumers in this transfer category need charitable advice—emotional advice on how to impact future generations whether through wealth or other training or mentoring. Digital-only platforms may figure out the deaccumulation stage, but we don't see any way for them to ever solve for the legacy transfer stage of the client life cycle. This stage requires advisors to deeply understand the emotional impacts of the client, and even with advancements in artificial intelligence, it's difficult to see how consumers embrace the digital assistance in this area.

THE CONSUMER PERSPECTIVE

Just as a widow or widower needs to hear a comforting voice after the loss of a spouse, there are other triggers that prompt a call to a financial advisor. It might be clients' realization that they have not saved enough for retirement, or even that it is time to start putting away money to reach that goal.

In an ideal world, consumers would connect with advisors long before they actually need to take any action. The best advice is delivered by an advisor when it has been built on the foundation of a relationship, not when it's reactionary. Even with the best possible advice, it's a lot more stressful if someone waits until a major life transition is already underway to get the planning process going. Lots of people think about investing for their infant's future college expenses, but financial advisors have limited tools available when the parent waits until a son or daughter is 16 to start discussing the investments to fund that education. Long-term care is the most serious example of waiting until it's too late to call for help. Planning for the care of an aging loved one really needs to start long before that person needs 24-hour assistance to get through the day.

In a world where consumers tend to seek advice at the point when the problem is upon them, or the moment they learn the financial world they've created is about to change. Gretchen, an oncology nurse who lives in suburban Boston, visited WealthRamp, founded by Pam Krueger, to connect with a financial advisor immediately after she was diagnosed with a serious long-term illness. Finding an advisor became Gretchen's top priority. Her husband, who works for MIT, had realized they would need to increase cash flow, and for this family, that meant selling the family home and moving into a much smaller house in an unfamiliar neighborhood. Although Gretchen wanted to enlist help from a qualified professional advisor, her husband wanted nothing to do with one. He'd had a string of negative experiences with brokers at major Wall Street firms, so the last thing he wanted was to get involved with yet another advisor who, he felt, would take advantage of them in this fragile state. The odds that Gretchen could find a trustworthy advisor online, in his opinion, were about the same as meeting up with the Tooth Fairy at the grocery store.

Yet with a daughter in high school and a son in college, this family needed expert financial planning advice to help them deal with a loss of one income and a life-threatening illness. They also needed an advisor to help them salvage a retirement lifestyle now hanging in the balance. Gretchen, on her own, came to Pam and WealthRamp with the hope of finding a financial planner who would guide them as they attempted to drastically downsize. Within 24 hours, they were put in touch with a financial planner near Boston, who the couple felt was a perfect fit for them. Gretchen followed up to report she and her very skeptical husband were relieved when they learned they could work through this, and that they would be all right as they took this step into the next chapter of their lives.

Every day, families have to deal with critically important financial decisions and situations that they never dreamed would crop up in their lives. Their stories are real and often serious, and in those instances, individuals are looking for a specialist, not an algorithm. They're not going to find convenient answers to these highly personal challenges by typing words and phrases into Google. Compare them with a couple who has a child with special needs and is in search of legal assistance. They won't be well served by using LegalZoom to tackle their unique estate planning.

When faced with these kinds of difficult situations, a financial advisor is probably not the first person to come to mind, but it is the right time to hit the reset button. Consumers may not understand exactly what financial planning is, but they clearly understand when they need to reach out for advice. For every one of us who encounters a divorce, an unexpected death or some other triggering point, we should at least be aware of the tools to find the Essential Advisor who can offer help.

These life events are the financial game-changers, and we believe advisors make themselves essential to clients by helping them through life transitions. They exist everywhere, their advice is affordable and they can be found if the consumer takes the appropriate steps to look for them.

KEY TAKEAWAYS

- Advice is most needed when the financial and emotional aspects of a consumer decision or circumstance intersect with each other.
- The Essential Advisor is able to identify where these intersections exist. Most likely they will occur when a consumer is going through some sort of transition in their life.
- The Essential Advisor will build their operating model around certain transitions and partner with other experts to provide outside expertise where necessary.
- The digital-only platforms have been good at serving clients in the accumulation stage of their life cycle. However, as consumers move to the deaccumulation and transfer cycles, the human advisor has a distinct advantage and is necessary. The emotions and relationship are too critical for digital-only advice.
- To assist a consumer through a transition takes time and emotional investment. Firms and practices will need to build technology and operating models that increase efficiencies to free up client-facing time.

CHAPTER 7

Success in the Digital Revolution

Even some of the greatest technology-led revolutions, or allegedly technology-led, really were only made possible because of trends already present.

—Scott Cook

Revolutions are often remembered as sudden, sweeping events that instantly impact the world, but in reality they usually are the culminating results of a series of small changes. The U.S. Declaration of Independence was written in two days, but had taken years of friction with the British crown to reach that turning point. Neil Armstrong stepped out of Apollo 11 eight years after President Kennedy first spoke boldly about going to the moon. The iPhone has drastically changed the way we communicate, but it came into existence decades into Steve Jobs's work to develop personal computers.

In the financial industry, we are not going through an *evolution*, but a *revolution*. The consumer is pushing the industry to think differently. The digital movement is pushing change quicker than ever and will continue to pick up the pace. Throughout this book, we have built the case that the Essential Advisor will create a strong value proposition focused on the consumer perspective, and put this at the center of their service. The digital revolution will lead the industry to bifurcate. It will cause an extreme difference between the great and average advisors, and much of this is going to come through how they manage and run their practices and their firms. In the wake of the digital revolution, success is going to hinge on a new approach to the client experience, including how advisors spend their time and how they create efficiencies to meet the continued demand for advice. Few advisors argue about whether the digital revolution exists, but not all have accepted what it means to their businesses. The hybrid model—a human and computer working together to apply their particular strengths—will always beat a computer or human working alone. Others have made this case, but they have left out a number of key variables. Throughout this chapter, we get specific about how we think the hybrid model should be built and delivered.

Some firms will need to fight hard to change the way they operate. We're reminded of the movie *The Martian*, where Matt Damon plays an astronaut who is stranded on Mars. His character, Mark Watney, makes this statement:

> At some point, everything's gonna go south on you and you're going to say, this is it. This is how I end. Now you can either accept that, or you can get to work. That's all it is. You just begin. You do the math. You solve one problem and you solve the next one, and then the next. And if you solve enough problems, you get to come home.

The future of financial advice isn't as dire as being left to fend for yourself on Mars, but advisors can focus on making small, incremental changes that will add up to a drastic shift in the way they serve their current and potential clients.

DATA, INSIGHTS, AND ADVICE

It seems like no matter where you look, data is the story. There's small data, which is manageable for humans to comprehend with typical data processing, and there's big data, which is too vast to make sense of without specialized applications. In both forms, data is especially trendy these days. The problem with all the talk is there's very little discussion about what all of this data can do for advisors and investors in very real terms. How do advisors harness data to help the consumer without adding to the noise? How do investors use data to improve their lives and improve their relationship with their advisors? We believe the Essential Advisor will find ways to use data to bring clarity to financial challenges and improve the consumer's decision-making process.

Not all data is created equal. Figure 7.1 depicts the way we believe data will underpin the delivery of good financial advice. At the foundation of the pyramid is *data* itself. Once the raw data is distilled into understandable units, it will be available to consumers on digital platforms such as personal computers and mobile phones. There, it will inform consumers about important facts of their financial lives, including spending, budgets, cash flow, and so on. An example of a data point will be, "You spent $55 last month at Starbucks." Consumers will be able to learn something about their behavior through the data, but as the advisor is able to provide the next level of experience,

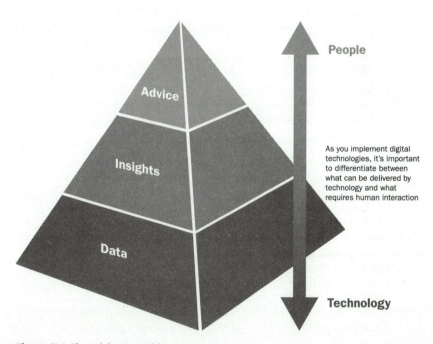

Figure 7.1 The Advice Pyramid

the value of the advisor rises. These *insights* build on the data to create the center of the pyramid. Using our coffee example, an advisor's insight might be communicated as, "You spent $55 last month at Starbucks, while the average consumer spent $35 and those in your zip code spent $30." As advisors provide insights, their relationships with consumers will become closer. Through this insight, consumers can understand the data in context, giving them the ability to understand an important spending habit relative to a benchmark.

Many people are wired to be competitive, so seeing the benchmarks for spending and other financial statistics will encourage certain behaviors. Jay is in that category, and he describes first-hand the power of benchmarking: "Each month our home energy provider benchmarks our usage versus the average home and the highly efficient home. They put those numbers on our bill right next to our own. Seeing those numbers makes me want to put on an extra sweater and turn the heat down so we can beat the benchmarks. My wife probably wonders if she married a lunatic." In addition to providing benchmarks, the energy company does something that is similar to what the top advisory firms do: They offer a consultation for homeowners who would like to adjust their energy consumption statistics. This is where the conversation shifts into the top part of the pyramid—*advice*. As consumers move up the advice pyramid from data to advice, they also rely more heavily on human interaction. To complete our Starbucks example, the consumer understands her discretionary coffee habit and has some context. Now, at the advice stage, she gets a ping from her advisor: "If you were to spend at the average level versus your current, you could put the difference in an investment account and it could equal $10,000 when you retire. Here are some investment solutions. Let's sit down and discuss." This opens the door to having a much more productive planning session to discuss the investor's retirement goals. It also brings the relationship beyond digital communication and into a face-to-face discussion.

As the investor moves up the advice pyramid, the digital platform enables the consumer and advisor to have a much deeper view of the consumer's financial situation. Much like a doctor using diagnostic tests to make medical recommendations, advisors are going to use data to make more informed suggestions about future financial decisions.

The hybrid model will allow the digital platform to inform through data and, as the consumer needs more complex solutions, the advice delivered by the human advisor completes the cycle of advice.

The Importance of Data Aggregation

We discussed in a prior chapter the lasting legacy of the robo movement. One key item referenced was the importance of data aggregation. The Essential Advisor isn't focused on only investable assets, but also on financial life management that supports consumers with budgeting, cash flow, debt, and insurance. The only way to be able to deliver on this future of holistic financial advice is by seeing the entire financial picture of the consumer in one place. Some advisors handle this manually by creating spreadsheets, typing in numbers from statements or various data sources and then uploading the data into a client vault. That's certainly better than nothing, but investors are beginning to expect real-time updates and a seamless experience on mobile devices. Data aggregation services make this entire process much simpler and keep firms compliant, allowing the client to maintain ownership of their login credentials.

There are two other key reasons to consider data aggregation an important pillar for future success. The first is the ability to grow share of wallet. Many investors have accounts all over the place because they've accumulated assets and investments through all types of relationships. They have a 401(k) account they never got around to rolling over when they left their last job. They have an investment account with a broker because they got tired of saying no when they golfed with him at the country club. They have another investment account because they wanted to help their nephew, who started working as a financial advisor, but now works at a financial technology company that enables investors to use emojis while building their portfolios. The advisors that can simplify the financial picture and provide advice on all of the accounts will not only make an impact on the lives of their clients, but they will also gain a larger share of wallet as consumers become comfortable consolidating assets and the relationship in one place. If you are a consumer, aren't you much more likely to do business with the advisor who can act like a quarterback of your financial life?

Data aggregation is good for the client and it's good for the advisor's business results. That should be reason enough to encourage any firm to incorporate data aggregation into their practice. Another reason to keep it top of mind is that your competition probably is. As you move up the curve in average client size, it is more likely for a consumer to have more than one financial advisor. Through data aggregation, the other advisors are seeing your accounts—and you can bet they chirp in your clients' ears about your performance and anything else they can see from the real-time automated statements. Without your own data aggregation, you cannot see what those advisors are up to, which puts you at a serious disadvantage.

THE FUTURE OF PLANNING

About two years ago we were on the phone with a broker talking about various things and the topic of financial planning came up. The broker quickly went out of his way to tell us that he did not create financial plans for his clients because he didn't believe in them. We encounter many investment managers who do not offer financial planning services, but this broker's reasoning was certainly uncommon. He told us, "Financial plans are meaningless because the clients never stick to what they need to stick to and the plan changes almost as soon as you complete it." By that reasoning, there's no reason to make your bed because you are going to sleep in it again; it's a waste of time to get your car washed because it's just going to get dirty again.

The flaw in this line of thinking has nothing to do with the concept of a financial plan, but in the broker's view of what is valuable for consumers. This broker's approach to the advisor-investor relationship might have made sense in 1995, and it can still make sense for a small set of the population, but we can guarantee that view of the world isn't going to make an advisor essential to the client of the future. As Elliot Weissbluth put it to us, "People do all kinds of crazy things to themselves. Just look at the number of crazy diets there are out there. People actually talk themselves into smoking to lose weight. Advisors will always be needed to save consumers from themselves." For this broker to say financial plans are worthless because people don't stick to them completely misses the opportunity and responsibility an advisor has to ensure clients follow through on the excellent advice that has been given.

There are absolutes in this world. The sky is blue, there are 24 hours in a day, and goal-based planning and reporting is the future of financial planning. Over the next decade, a majority of future consumers will not work with advisors that cannot deliver real-time planning. The financial information gained through data aggregation will feed goal-based reporting systems, allowing investors to see in real time where they stand against the attainment of their goals.

Some readers may wonder how automated this financial planning process will be and how this future aligns with our thesis that good financial advisors are going to be more relevant in the future as a result of the digital revolution. The vision of digital real-time, goals-based financial planning seems like it could be completed by a digital platform without a human advisor. For certain consumers that may be so, but there are some key items missing from the digital-only platforms.

For all the benefits goal-based planning can bring to the consumer experience, it can also bring confusion. We've been on the front lines with organizations trying to roll out goal-based financial planning, and two consistent consumer questions keep coming to the forefront:

1. How many goals should I have?
2. How do I understand how my goals interact with each other and the choices and tradeoffs I need to make?

Answering these questions is not a simple exercise. The right answer will only come from a clear understanding of many variables, both emotional and financial. The most common conversation about tradeoffs concerns funding education or retirement. Many investors come to this crossroads if they are underfunded for their children's college education, especially if they are unlucky enough to have the market tank during a child's freshman year in college. The question becomes, "Should we hold off for a period of time in funding the retirement goal to more fully fund college, or do we think differently about what we do for our kids?" The Essential Advisor is able to sit down with a family and navigate the goal and funding tradeoffs. Fully informed by a digital financial planning platform, the advisor will be empowered to have a deep conversation where relationships are built and an immense amount of value is delivered.

Advisors and consumers need to be aware of what some of the leading firms are doing in the area of financial planning. One company on the cutting edge of changing the definition of financial planning is United Capital, led by CEO Joe Duran. United Capital's self-described purpose as a company is to become the largest "financial life management" company in the country. They are taking goal-based financial planning and stretching it even further. Duran described to us why: "People need three things from their advisor: to ensure their money is helping them live a meaningful life, to ensure their investments are doing what they need to be doing to support the first goal, and to provide peace of mind when big things happen that everything is going to be okay." United Capital has built a number of technology tools into a sophisticated client portal, but two items are especially worth noting. They believe a financial advisor is much more than "financial" and that the advisor needs to help consumers live their lives the way they wish to attain satisfaction. It's important for the advisor to understand what this picture looks like. Once the picture is understood, activities are created and the consumer at any point in time can go onto a digital portal and assess how they feel about their current life activities. Based on their answers, they get an "Ideal Life Index" score out of 100. Over time, United Capital's clients can track their progress in trying to lead a more satisfying life. It also gives the advisor the opportunity to engage or find patterns where the clients do not appear to be making progress or have gone backward. This index allows advisors and investors to find those transition or infliction points where advice or collaboration may be needed. The tool also allows spouses to collaborate or complete the exercise independently of each other.

United Capital also believes technology interactions with consumers can bring peace of mind. On their client portal they've brought in the concept of "Years of Freedom." The planning tool takes a client balance sheet and shows them, based on spending goals, how many years they can be okay with no additional income. Getting clients to understand that they really are safe even when market volatility or other tough situations pop up goes a long way to making them sleep at night. This is not going to work for every advisor and consumer because some don't wish to have this deep type of relationship, but for the ones that do, it's hard to argue that this process isn't what "essential" looks like in the future. United Capital's acceptance of the digital revolution, where technology tools can not only inform the advisor and consumer but also increase the experience, is the exact hybrid model that is going to drive the future of advice.

CHANGE THE MEETING

Embracing the digital revolution will allow advisors to become essential by changing the way they design client meetings. Most client meetings today seem to go like this:

- Advisor asks about how things are doing, that last vacation, kids, upcoming wedding, and so on.
- Advisor talks through a market outlook and their view on the market.
- Advisor talks through some reports with the benchmarks and performance.
- Client asks a few questions and the meeting ends.

This is not an oversimplification.

The meetings for the Essential Advisor of the future aren't going to look like this at all. The meetings are going to be more meaningful and less frequent. Consumers don't want to spend hours with their advisor once a quarter. They are going to be more involved by using the digital client portals to stay informed between meetings. The advisor will be able to cater to the client by providing relevant, desirable information, and the client will be able to do the same. News, investment performance reports, updated financial plans, tax documents, estate documents will all be available in real time and in one place.

The Essential Advisor is going to reach out to a client two weeks in advance of a meeting to talk through the agenda. The agenda is going to be customized to address the concerns of the client and other key planning topics, not just investment performance. The clients will come to the meeting already knowing what the accounts are doing because they either went online to the client portal by themselves or the advisor pinged them to do so. The goal: to remove performance of assets as the center point of the meeting.

The meeting now looks like this:

- The advisor is aware the client's child just went away to school, which is the start of the conversation.

- The advisor then says, "I was thinking about the legal documents you have in place. Now that your child is away at school and is 18 years old, do you have a health-care power of attorney and did you sign HIPAA forms? If not, when your child gets sick the medical personnel and school can't talk to you as the parent. We should talk to your attorney and make sure they get updated." Imagine the value in that conversation. That's essential planning.

- The advisor and client review the financial plan and track in real time four goals that were in place from the last meeting. Tradeoffs, if needed, are discussed or, even better, the clients see they are on a trajectory to reach their goals. One of the goals is to take the entire family on a European vacation two years out. The advisor shows them they are on track and even offers to make an introduction to one of three travel agencies the firm has a relationship with to assist in the travel plans.

- The final item is the review of the client portal and communication. The advisor divides his or her practice into four communication-frequency buckets (e.g., a lot, a little, and two levels in between). If you are a level 4 you get everything— blog links, trade explanations, market outlooks, and weekly news. If you are level 1 you get very little, as you have chosen to more largely delegate to the advisor. The client and advisor discuss how often and what types of communication the client wishes to receive and they set the client portal to align with this information. The meeting ends with each side being very clear on the level of expected communication between meetings.

ESSENTIAL ADVISOR PRINCIPLE NO. 4

The Essential Advisor communicates clearly, truthfully, and consistently.

Platform of the Future

We spoke earlier in book about the error in assuming the stand-alone robo-advisor movement is the future. We believe the digital revolution is the extension of the current advisor operating model. The Essential Advisor will build technology that will offer the ability for a 20-year-old do-it-yourselfer all the way to a 70-year-old retired couple wanting a deep relationship with a human advisor and everyone in between to do business with the firm or practice. The weakness of firms in the past has been the inability to use technology to cater processes and deliver advice around different client experiences. The platforms today and into the future give advisors the ability to interact and cater the client experience across multiple desires, not just one.

ESSENTIAL ADVISOR PRINCIPLE NO. 5

The Essential Advisor tailors communication, education, and the overall client experience to meet the unique needs, style, and concerns of each client.

The Long View of the Digital Revolution

We've included some comments from our interview with Ric Edelman throughout the book, but his ideas on the future of the digital revolution were the most eye opening. Ric believes the digital revolution is going to extend much further than anyone we talked with in the writing of this book. He ties the technology advances in the wider economy, especially health care, with the digital revolution in financial services. He believes as our clients live longer, their ability to retrain themselves for continued changes in the job market will be key to staying employed and maintain a lifestyle much longer than the ones sustained today. He also believes longevity is going to cause differences in longer-term living arrangements. The advisor of the future will need to assist clients with career planning

(Continued)

(*Continued*)

and training as well as planning around longer-term living arrangements. This is a very long view of the industry and we'll need to wait for quite a while to see if this prediction plays out. However, the reason we included this discussion is because it underscores a key outcome of the digital revolution: Regardless of the advances in technology, the areas where advice is needed might change, but the fact that advice is needed won't go away even in one of the longest views of the industry.

UNDERSTAND THE COST OF IMPLEMENTATION

When someone pays an advisor they aren't generally paying for one thing, they are actually paying for two things: the advice itself and the implementation of that advice. When you go to an estate-planning attorney, she tells you how to structure your estate and then creates the documents. When you go to a CPA, he advises you on how to structure your return and then files it. When a financial advisor provides advice, whether it's planning or investment advice, that advice has to be implemented in some way. If you step back and think about what the robo advisors have done, it is very similar to what the discount brokers did to the trading business years ago: They have driven down the cost of implementation. We will review fees in greater detail in the next chapter, but the robo advisor platforms have driven down the cost of implementing advice and passed some of that savings onto the end consumer in cheaper fees. Of all the arguments for the hybrid model of the future, this serves as the foundational issue. For advisors to compete, they need to aggressively drive down their cost of implementation, likely through the use of digital technology. Without doing so, the consumer value equation is going to be off because the best firms are going to be investing their resources in the delivery of advice and the experience related to the delivery of advice for the consumer. Firms not doing so will be left behind. Consumers will be willing to pay more for an enhanced client experience. Consumers will be willing to pay for more effective communication. Consumers will no longer be willing to pay firms that spend more time implementing advice than giving it. It's that simple.

Drive Down the Cost of Implementation

The Essential Advisor will fight issues brought on by the cost of implementation by getting extremely efficient with their time. If you are an advisor, do you know where you spend your time in a given week? To find out how you *really* spend it, chart your time for two weeks by color coding your calendar, using one color for time actually spent with clients, one color for time actually spent with prospects, one color for internal activities, and the last color for time spent getting ready for meetings or doing follow-up's from them. After two weeks, you will quickly see whether you spend more time delivering advice or implementing it. Most advisors we have done this exercise with are surprised when they get to the end of the two weeks. They spend a lot less time with clients than they believe they do.

Driving down the cost of implementation means focusing on technology and on some very key areas in the advice delivery process:

1. Financial planning: Completing plans in real time with very little manual input.

2. On-boarding new clients: The new client on-boarding process is one area where manual processes cause significant leakage in time spent. Data aggregation is going to be key to avoid the manual process of inputting account holdings into a proposal system.

3. Trading: We've mentioned this before, but we want to be absolutely clear. Unless you are running small-cap equity, derivatives, or certain fixed-income portfolios, the advisor provides little value in trading. Use technology.

4. Meeting preparation: If you are an advisor, do the math on the number of meetings you do in a year. Let's say it's seven per week for 48 weeks a year or 336 meetings a year. One of the biggest areas where efficiency can be gained is the time it takes to get ready for a meeting. Firms lose a lot of time when their CRM systems aren't integrated or when their reporting packages for the meeting are very manual. If the average client meeting takes two hours to prepare for and that time is cut in half, the advisor gains around eight weeks of productivity. Imagine the number of key transitions an advisor could help clients through with eight extra weeks of productivity.

An advisor last week got into an argument with us and said technology wasn't important because labor in the back office is cheap. He actually referred to his back office as *hamsters*, which is interesting in its own right, but argued he could just continue to add more. This has diminishing returns as people have to be hired, trained, and managed. Why would an advisor spend their time doing these functions instead of spending time with clients? The Essential Advisor of the future will be spending time with clients.

ESSENTIAL ADVISOR PRINCIPLE NO. 6
The Essential Advisor uses technology to maximize the value of the time spent with clients.

The Weakness of Being in the Technology Business

Many advisors are feeling the pressure of the digital revolution because they are approaching it as if they now need to be in the "technology business." The advancement of the technology solutions that exist in the marketplace is astounding and the pace at which they continue to change sometimes surprises even us—and we do this for a living. The consumer feels the same pressure. What the digital revolution has done for the industry is extremely positive. It's brought not only the benefits to the consumer as we'd previously reviewed, but it's also brought immense amounts of capital to the financial services sector, which gives advisors a chance to utilize technology to literally do almost anything they want. The negative of the amount of technology coming to the industry is it's easy to overbuy or to overdesign it. There are a lot of financial technology companies creating technology solutions that don't solve a problem that currently exists. We saw one recently where an investor can search for stock symbols using the emoji, the picture icons on their phones. There're probably aren't 10 people in the entire world that think something like that is needed. Advisors need to spend time with clients, they need to spend time with prospects trying to grow their businesses and as a result they don't need to be in the technology business. The advantage of the digital revolution is there are a large number of great companies out there allowing the advisors to grab off-the-shelf technology and bring it to the business in a much less disruptive manner than previously existed. If you want to grow your business in through the digital revolution invest in technology, but don't fool yourself into needing to be in the technology business. Whether you are a consumer or an advisor, you won't keep up. Sit down and simply lay out what's important to you and your business and stay focused on investing in those areas. Don't let the bells and whistles overcomplicate it.

OVERCOMING THE LACK OF LONG-TERM TECHNOLOGY ADOPTION

The Essential Advisor is going to differentiate him- or herself by bucking the trends of past technology adoption. Historically a large percentage of the advisor population would implement new technology, generally only if it helped in the new client acquisition or development area. The parts of the technology that would help advisors win new clients would be utilized and the rest of it would be largely ignored. The Essential Advisor will ride the digital revolution and digitize their back offices. They will seamlessly integrate their CRM systems with their platforms for trading, reporting, and managing documents. The manual processes are going to be too expensive going forward. In 2013, the independent consulting firm Aite completed a study to look at the efficiencies of registered independent firms with integrated technology platforms versus those without an integrated platform. The firms with an integrated platform were 32 percent more efficient, freeing up almost 40 hours per year of staff time to be focused more on client-facing activities. This free time correlated to outstanding growth and increased income with the integrated firms generating 18 percent more revenue with integration than without. This increased revenue provides increased cash flow to invest in technology, people, and the overall client experience. This continued investment will be important to staying essential.

 THE CONSUMER PERSPECTIVE

Everyone has been at one of those meetings where they wish an oxygen mask would fall from the ceiling to keep us awake. The meeting has no agenda, and nothing really gets done. Although people put up with those kinds of meetings at work, the

(Continued)

(*Continued*)

last thing consumers want is to waste their valuable time with their eyes glazing over when they come in for answers from their financial advisor.

Consumers will feel they are getting their money's worth if they know that their advisor has thought ahead and prepped for their meeting by providing a simple agenda. The agenda helps consumers focus on their highest priorities and gives them a chance to participate in the conversation instead of sitting back listening to a lecture about stock market volatility. Consumers get it. They read the headlines. The stock market is volatile. Now show me how much it impacts the likelihood that I'll still reach my goals.

Pam Krueger, an investor advocate, asked several users on WealthRamp how they felt about answering all of the questions she asks in order to match them with the right advisor, and she recognized that consumers would view some of the questions as rather intrusive. Here's what wealthy user named Rosalind told Pam about WealthRamp's invasive questions:

> I've just gone through this huge divorce proceeding. I needed to answer these questions, and you made it easy. You asked me to single out every aspect of my financial life that mattered to me. And when I actually saw ALL of MY priorities stacked up as brightly colored balls in the bins staring back at me, I then knew WHY I needed an advisor and what kind of advisor I needed to find.

Most consumers want their advisors to have access to all of their relevant information gathered from every available source. More importantly, they want their advisor to understand their vision—their *ideal life index.* When an advisor understands that person's ideal life index, the client's comfort level is likely to escalate rapidly. Clients will feel more confident if their advisor is knowledgeable about their priorities based upon the big picture, not just a snapshot of one investment account. It's a disservice to both the advisor and the client if decisions are based on only one piece of the puzzle. It would be like hiring a therapist but limiting what you share about your life. At WealthRamp, Pam recently worked with a consumer in Oklahoma who appeared to have a modest amount of assets, but she wanted to learn more about investing by working with an advisor. After probing more deeply, the advisor quickly found out that the real reason she wanted to learn more about investing was because she and her husband were about to come into a windfall from an invention worth tens of millions that they were about to sell to an oil company.

When advisors do know every aspect of a client's finances, they can pull together the right team. As an example, the client might benefit from tax expertise and trust services. This approach lifts the weight off the individual's shoulders and strengthens the advisor-client bond.

As she matches consumers with advisors, Pam is asking both of them how they prefer to interact and communicate with each other. For example, she asks investors to rate on a scale of one to five the following types of questions:

- Are you the type of consumer who expects your advisor to handle all of the details or do you want to know the rationale for every decision?

- Do you expect to hear from your advisor at least once a month and every time the smallest issue crops up?

- How do you prefer to communicate? Are you happy with talking twice a year as long as you're satisfied everything's in order?

Some consumers want to hear from their advisor via e-mail, while others really expect a phone call or a face-to-face meeting. While performance is important, misfiring on these communication touch points is the primary reason, just after performance, for why clients fire their advisor.

A lot of individual investors, and not just the younger ones, want an advisor who uses robust, high-tech tools. Someone in his mid-forties is likely to ask if you can generate a highly personalized report that will show him the future of his cash flow based on certain assumptions. For example, as a follow-up to a face-to-face meeting, the consumers Pam has met are asking if they can see a report that shows them "what if" scenarios and the best way for them to maximize their Social Security benefits. Consumers can walk away with a much better understanding of advisory fees whenever they can see evidence of the advisor's planning efforts.

KEY TAKEAWAYS

- The industry is going through a *revolution*, not an *evolution*. To keep pace with the speed of change, the industry's necessary operational shifts will continue to accelerate.

- The Essential Advisors of the future are going to aggressively focus on client service instead of on implementing advice.

- The digital platforms of the top firms will need to stretch to serve a wide number of client experiences.

- The top advisors in the future are going to master communication, customizing content and touchpoints to the exact needs of each client.

■ It's expensive and time consuming to be in the technology business. Firms and advisors will need to partner with technology-focused companies to stay ahead of the changing landscape and focus their time on client-service activities.

CHAPTER 8

Maximizing Value

Price is what you pay. Value is what you get.

—Warren Buffett

Afew months ago we were asked to visit members of a firm to discuss how they might increase revenue. They focused on investment management and were having a difficult time differentiating themselves from the rise of the digital advice providers. We had a long discussion about how the firm charged fees and it became quite clear they had overcomplicated the process. One comment that stood out came from their chief compliance officer, who said, "We discount a lot." After the meeting, we asked them to give us their fee schedules and their last billing file so we could analyze what was happening. One of our analysts reviewing the files realized that they were discounting significantly, and in some cases they weren't charging their clients *at all*. It's common for us to see friend and family discounts, but it's very rare to see clients charged no fees at all. One of the firm's fee-free clients had $30 million with the advisor. Given even *low* industry averages, this client should have been paying $125,000 or more annually, so the firm was leaving a lot of money on the table. We went back to the owners with the $30 million example and asked why they were not charging any fees on that account. The answer was one of the most amazing things we had ever heard: "If we charge them, they might leave." This firm was providing services to a client for *free*, which effectively resulted in a net loss because of the time and resources spent managing such a large account. Despite this, they were concerned the client might leave, which would result in the same revenue, less work, and far less legal risk. From our perspective, that would not be such a bad outcome. This firm had no confidence in itself and the value it was bringing to its clients. In the absence of value, of course, a client wouldn't pay, but this firm was devaluing its services so much it didn't even want to ask clients for basic fees. This is an extreme example, but it happens more often than you would think. As we referenced in Chapter 5, there are a lot of firms that should be worried about their value propositions but aren't. A firm that doesn't charge clients because it thinks they might leave the practice definitely needs to worry and should start developing a new value proposition right away.

This story also points out a key issue with many firms and the industry. We tend to measure success based on a single metric—assets under management (AUM)—that has little correlation to the actual financial success of our businesses. When you walk around conferences, nobody talks in terms of *revenue*; instead, they always refer to *assets*. AUM correlates to the success of a firm, but much less than revenue. This firm feels good about not charging its $30 million client because that client adds $30 million to the firm's AUM, despite there being no business outcome to show for it. That $30 million in assets under management isn't paying the rent or making payroll. To remain essential to consumers in the future, it will take continued investments in people and technology. Those investments come from cash flow derived from revenue, not from AUM.

IS THE COST OF ADVICE PROHIBITIVE?

A recent survey identified the cost of advice as a top concern for those Americans thinking about talking to a financial advisor. According to a study from McAdam, an independent financial planning firm, 71 percent of Americans are afraid working with a financial advisor will end up costing them a lot of money.[1] The title of McAdam's press release

---

[1] McAdam, LLC, "Financial Advisor-Phobia: 71 Percent of Americans Say They Are Scared of Talking to a Financial Advisor," Marketwired, October 27, 2015, www.marketwired.com/press-release/financial-advisor-phobia-71-percent-americans-say-they-are-scared-talking-financial-2067524.htm.

makes the point quite bluntly: "Financial Advisor-Phobia: 71 Percent of Americans Say They Are Scared of Talking to a Financial Advisor."

Even respondents with higher incomes were concerned about the cost of talking to a financial advisor. Almost 40 percent said they were fearful the financial advisor would give them bad news.

According to a study prepared by State Street Global Advisors, investors want to have open, honest relationships with their financial advisors and they want to trust them, but investors' confusion about fees gets in the way. One-third of investors do not understand the fees or commission they are charged. This confusion causes them to be dubious of and less satisfied with their financial advisors.[2]

The State Street Global Advisors study also found that investors do not object to paying for financial advice. They do, however, want a clear understanding of what they are paying and what they receive in return. Clients expect to see a *return* on an advisor's advice, and we don't necessarily mean *investment* returns. It is imperative for advisors to discuss their fees and value propositions with confidence and clarity. The ability to do so will help advisors gain their clients' trust and advocacy. No matter how advisory firms structure their fees, they need to create an ongoing dialog with clients in order to build stronger bonds.[3]

The study concluded that fees are rarely the reason why clients terminate a relationship with a financial advisor. When clients leave a firm, their departure is often triggered by problems with communication or trust.

Human versus Robot

In a world where people pay $5 for a cup of coffee, value selling will always be alive. One of the lasting impacts of the stand-alone robo-advisor movement is that it has refocused consumers on costs and transparency. However, robo advisors have not redirected focus onto *value* and this is a key differentiation consumers and advisors should

---

[2] "The Price of Financial Advice," State Street Global Advisors, www.spdru.com/content-kits/the-price-of-financial-advice-ck.

[3] "The Price of Financial Advice: Communicating Fee Value Proposition with Clarity," State Street Global Advisors, http://isectors.com/wp-content/uploads/2015/08/The_Price_of_Financial_Advice.pdf.

understand. Let's do a quick exercise to show the difference. For the sake of this exercise, let's define the term *net value* as the *cost of advice* subtracted from the *value an advisor delivers*:

Net Value = Value Delivered – Cost of Advice

A positive net value means the value of advice exceeds the amount of fees paid. In the end, net value is what a client should care about. It answers the questions: What was the value I received compared to what I paid for the current advisory model? How does this compare to other models out there?

Recall Chapter 4's Capital Sigma review, where we explain how good advice can create more than 300 basis points of value per year for the end investor. This concept is centered on the five pillars of value: financial planning, asset class selection and allocation, investment vehicle selection, systematic rebalancing, and tax management. We use this same methodology to calculate the net value of financial advice. To do this, we follow four simple steps:

1. **Score each of the pillars**. Assign basis points to reflect the total potential value the advisor can deliver on each one. (If you have trouble with this, revisit Chapter 4.)

2. **Find the total value**. Add the scores of the five pillars together to determine the total potential value the advisor generates. This number becomes the *value delivered* in your net value equation.

3. **Find the total cost.** Determine the total cost of the advice, again using basis points. This number becomes the *cost of advice* in your net value equation.

4. **Calculate the net value.** Subtract the cost of advice (Step 3) from the total value delivered (Step 2).

Figure 8.1 uses this calculation to pit human advisors head to head against robo advisors. For this analysis, we went through the five pillars of Capital Sigma and first made a note of the total potential value in basis points of each one. Then, based on our research, we divided these points between the average human and robo advisor to reflect the value each one brings to the consumer.

In this exercise, we assumed that a client would want all five pillars of value, including financial planning and coaching, Pillar 1. We

Pillar of Value	Winner	Potential Value[1]	Robo Net Value	Human Net Value
Financial Planning	Human	64	0	64
Asset Class Selection and Allocation	Tie	28	14	14
Investment Vehicle Selection	Tie	80	40	40
Systematic Rebalance	Robo	44	22	22
Tax Management	Tilted to Human	100	25	75
Average Advice Fees[2]			(45)	(100)
Net Value Created			56	115

Figure 8.1 A Calculation of Net Value

[1]From Capital Sigma Research and Envestnet ENVESTAT Research. Amounts in basis points. See Chapter 4 for more details.
[2]Calculated using industry averages of observed advice fees.

assigned the full score value of Pillar 1 to human advisors, as their planning and coaching potential far outpaces that of robots. We considered the area of asset class selection and allocation to be a tie, so we assigned half of the basis points for this pillar to each advisor type. We also considered humans and robots to be equal in terms of investment vehicle selection, so we also split the points equally for this pillar. In the area of rebalancing we also considered this area a tie. For the tax management pillar, we gave one-quarter of the points to robots and three-quarters to humans. Some robo advisors provide tax-aware offerings, but we believe human intervention is needed to capture most of the value in this very complex area.

We wanted to make this data as binary as possible to provide a true apples-to-apples comparison, assuming a consumer would choose to work with either a digital-only solution or a human model. For example, a human could provide rebalancing services but, as we mentioned in Chapter 5, this is one area that is best left to robots. A hybrid advisory model might reallocate some of these basis points, but due to the variety and complexity of hybrid models, we have left them out of this table.

Once our values were in place, we began to calculate the cost of human and robo advice. To do this, we relied on industry averages and pricing data we have observed. The analysis excludes *product* costs, what a consumer would pay for investment vehicles such as mutual funds and ETFs. Product costs are the same whether portfolios are managed by humans or robots, so they do not impact the value delivered *directly by the advisor* to the end consumer. In the end, the human advisor edges out the robot when it comes to value—despite costing more than twice as much.

This analysis is for illustrative purposes only, but the results point out some foundational issues:

- Both robo advisors and well-executed human advice provide a positive net value to consumers. Consumers will receive value that is worth more than the fees they pay in this scenario and across many scenarios.

- It's not about only cost, but also service. Part of the reason robo advisors have lower fees is that they provide fewer services. For consumers wanting deep tax-management and financial-planning expertise, they are typically paying a human advisor for it and, in most cases, not paying a robo advisor. This is one reason for the significant gap in the cost of advice. Robot advice isn't just cheaper—it has less to offer, and what it does include is often conducted at a lower level of service.

- This exercise shows why robo advisors are good for some consumers, generally those who are younger. In many cases, younger consumers have fewer assets and they likely have fewer planning and tax management needs. The planning and tax-management pillars account for a large chunk of overall value. If you rerun this analysis with only the investment management categories (Pillars 2, 3, and 4), the robo advisor would have a higher net value score than the human advisor.

- This analysis ignores the peace-of-mind argument, which is the most important point of all. We can assign quantitative scores to reflect the performance of different pillars of value, but the greatest value an advisor provides is peace of mind. When robo advisors advertise, they say, "You are paying too much." They talk about this wide gap of costs between their services and those of human advisors. Hopefully, this analysis shows that the gap in value delivered is certainly not as wide as stated. Consumers need to determine if they value the peace of mind that comes from picking up the phone and calling someone who knows them. We think it is.

ESSENTIAL ADVISOR PRINCIPLE NO. 7

The Essential Advisor helps the investor understand and manage the costs—including taxes—that come with investing.

Different Approaches to Charging Fees

We see all kinds of interesting fee schedules out there. When advisors are just starting out or hit a dry spell in attracting clients, they consider what they feel are innovative marketing ideas. There are a lot of different approaches out there. Occasionally, you will find an advisor who offers a satisfaction guarantee to new clients. If the client is not happy with the advisor's services, he or she does not need to pay a fee. We don't know how those promotions work out, but there is one thing we are sure of: Regulators may object to that approach because it might cause the firm to take excessive risks with the client's money.

A FIRM THAT RAISED FEES

No matter what the product or service, consumers can almost always find a better price. Sometimes this means making a sacrifice in brand, model, or quality. For instance, someone who loves music might be able to find a less expensive type of headphones that deliver satisfactory sound quality. When it comes to services, whether they are hiring a plumber, electrician, or a lawyer, consumers can always find someone who will do the work for a cheaper price. Some consumers go a step further and decide to save money by doing the work themselves. More than likely, there is a YouTube video that will show them how to perform the plumbing or electrical work. For legal services, consumers might turn to the Internet for general advice and templated forms they can adapt to create wills and contracts. None of this guarantees people will be happy with the end result.

For example, consider a consumer who is shopping for a new car. He or she can choose from a range of vehicles, from the most expensive new models to the cheapest clunkers on the used car lot, but they may not be satisfied with their driving experience. Additionally, there are many instances when a more expensive car holds its value longer, which translates to a better resale or trade-in price in the future. This type of value tradeoff can help defray the costs, making a pricier car a better deal. Like cars, there are many cases when a more expensive product can be a better value—especially if the cheaper alternative doesn't last as long as we anticipate.

Today, the discussion around fees tends to be mostly about their decline, but that isn't the case 100 percent of the time. You may remember, earlier in the book we referred to Jim Pratt-Heaney, a cofounder of LLBH Private Wealth Management. When talking to Pratt-Heaney about fees, we learned he's an outlier—his firm recently raised their fees instead of lowering them. The motivation behind that decision is that he believed the firm was providing more value and a wider service menu than they were getting paid for. We asked him if he was worried clients would leave. "At first, you always are a little apprehensive," he said, "but we were confident we were providing value and we kept reminding ourselves of the impact our clients were telling us we were making in their lives." In the end, LLBH had few issues when they raised fees—their clients saw the value.

A key part of a conversation about fees to recognize that clients are busy and it's easy for them to move through their daily lives without realizing the value and impact of the services their advisors provide. They forget what advisors do for them, so advisors need to remind them. Pratt-Heaney talked about a client who was chirping about fees. This client wouldn't have made it through a divorce financially without the assistance of the firm, so Pratt-Heaney prepared a very detailed summary of all of the things the firm had done for the client and his family. When the family saw it, they were floored. They knew the firm was an important part of their lives, but when they were reminded in great detail of the extent of their services, the fee discussion went away. If you are an advisor, consider how often you summarize what you are doing for a client. If you are a consumer, have you asked for this as part of the review process? Both parties should understand what is truly being accomplished. It's the only way a relationship can be built on value.

ADAPTING TO CHANGES IN FEE DISCLOSURE

When Seth Meyers hosted the White House Correspondents' Dinner in 2011, he jokingly criticized Congress for passing legislation without reading it. "I think you guys vote on bills in the same way the rest of us agree to updated terms and conditions on iTunes," Meyers observed.[4] At the time of Meyers's monologue, 56 pages of terms and conditions appeared when a user attempted to download music for the first time after an update. Anyone who uses software has at some point been faced with a similar terms-and-conditions box—and most of us click "Accept" without actually looking at what we are agreeing to. The stacks of paper investors sign when they enter into a financial arrangement with an advisor has historically gone much the same way; but that's changing. According to a recent report from Cerulli Associates, *high-net-worth investors view fee transparency as the most important differentiating feature among advice providers.*

Fee transparency is coming to the forefront. Digital advice platforms use it as a selling point, arguing that robo advisors are targeting their advertisements to younger consumers so pricing pressure won't come upstream. When Wealthfront ran a Super Bowl commercial that took advisory firms to task for high fees, people took notice. And you had better believe that higher-end clients pay attention to Schwab commercials (aired endlessly during golf tournaments) that push clients to ask advisors about fees.

We discussed fee transparency with Knut A. Rostad, president of the Institute for the Fiduciary Standard. According to Rostad, "Fee transparency is urgent in this environment of 1930s-level investor distrust of financial advisors. Opaque fees breed distrust, and, advisors must compete with seemingly transparent and far less costly digital platforms. In order to attract and retain clients, it is urgent that advisors be completely transparent in their fees. Otherwise, it will be impossible

---

[4] Umika Pidaparthy, "What You Should Know about iTunes' 56-Page Legal Terms," CNN .com, May 6, 2011, www.cnn.com/2011/TECH/web/05/06/itunes.terms/.

for advisors to keep their clients from peeling away—much less attract new clients."

For those readers who are not aware of the Institute for the Fiduciary Standard, it is a think tank and was founded in 2011. The Institute's single purpose is to promote the vital importance of the fiduciary standard in investment and financial advice. We don't want to get into a debate in this book about the "F word" (fiduciary). It is, however, relevant to see what the institute has published in 2016 about its view on best practices relating to fees. It's important advisors and consumers know what thoughts are being added to the debate about advisory fees:

- Provide a written statement of total fees and underlying investment expenses paid by the client. At the bare minimum, provide clients with instructions to obtain this information. Include any payments to the advisor, firm, or related parties, including those from any third-party resulting from the advisor's recommendations.

- While improvements have come about, the industry remains too opaque when it comes to underlying investment fees and expenses. The purpose of providing fee statements is to increase transparency and consumer awareness of investment expenses, which are not always readily apparent. This requires tallying or estimating underlying investments.

- Increasing expense transparency is challenging. Certain expenses (e.g., mutual fund expense ratios) are readily available while others are more difficult to determine. Depending on the type, some of these expenses may be calculated or estimated. Additionally, certain expenses may not be either calculated or reliably estimated, so advisors must rely on reported figures. An annual investment expense report may include a combination of these different types of expenses.

- Advisor fees include asset management fees and, if applicable, separate financial planning fees. Underlying investment expenses, as in the case of mutual funds, typically include the expense ratio and management fees, transaction fees, and custody fees. Depending on the share class, commissions, front-end or back-end loads, 12b-1 fees, and wrap fees may be included.

- Underlying investment expenses can be reported in a variety of ways. The first is through an accounting of the actual expenses associated with the investments. The second is with a good-faith estimate of the underlying expenses that includes a brief explanation of the basis. If neither of these methods are feasible, this practice may be met through an accounting and/or estimation of a typical firm portfolio with allocations that resemble, but most assuredly are not the same as, the client's.

- Alternatively, the advisor may fulfill this practice by assisting the client in obtaining the underlying investment expenses through a third-party vendor, such as Morningstar or FeeX. An advisor may also help the client calculate the investment expenses. In either case, the advisor's duty is to take reasonable care to assist the client in obtaining the necessary information for the annual report.

- The written statement of fees and expenses should be compiled no less often than annually.

ESSENTIAL ADVISOR PRINCIPLE NO 8

The Essential Advisor is comfortable talking to clients about fees, and is confident in the value provided for those fees.

Having *the Talk* with Clients and Prospects

At various points in life, all of us must have *the talk*—an uncomfortable conversation about a key relationship or fact of life. Like the talk parents have with their children about the birds and the bees, or the talk with an elderly father to tell him that his driving days are over, *the talk* between financial advisors and their clients is just as unappealing. Most financial advisors are especially squeamish about discussing fees with prospective clients because it happens at a point when the prospect does not know the advisor well and isn't quite convinced the firm will deliver on its value proposition. We think having *champions* is one way to make this conversation go more smoothly. *Champions* are current clients who are

(Continued)

(Continued)

willing to talk to prospects about the value an advisor provides. This can bridge the topic of fees with that of value by allaying investors' fears and convincing them there will be a return on advice. Champions support the value proposition and help clients understand that the advisor's fees are worth paying, and they will benefit from the expenditure.

Don't overcomplicate anything to create the appearance of value. Demonstrating the value proposition for clients does not require a financial advisor to make investing and financial planning complicated. A financial advisor should be able to explain the firm's strategy or its financial planning recommendations without making it seem like brain surgery.

There is no need for an advisor to convince clients that they cannot handle their own financial planning or investment management. Many clients hire advisors because they *don't want* to do it themselves. Advisors do not need to make financial planning seem more sophisticated than it actually is so consumers will hire them.

Similarly, advisors do not need to twist the truth to make their fees more palatable to the consumer. Some advisors consistently tell their clients, "We don't make money if you don't make money," even if that isn't accurate. We've heard advisors say this, then charge a percentage of AUM so clients pay a fee even if their accounts plummet in value. It would have been much more accurate for advisors to say their firms make more money when the client makes money, because the account goes up in value and the AUM increases significantly.

How the Oracle Discloses Fees

This all seems so simple, but it's not. Even the great Warren Buffett weighed in on how advisors should disclose fees and make things simpler. Buffett wrote the preface to the *Plain English Handbook*, which was published by the SEC. In the preface, Buffett said that when writing Berkshire Hathaway's annual report, the legendary investor pretends that he is talking to his sisters. Buffett recommended that people write with a specific person in mind and avoid technical jargon. The plainspoken Buffett summed up his approach by saying, "My goal is simply to give them the information I would wish them to supply me if our positions were reversed. To succeed, I don't need to be Shakespeare; I must, though, have a sincere desire to inform." Most of us will not invest as successfully as Warren Buffett. Nevertheless, we can all aspire to write and communicate with our clients as clearly as he does.

The Future of Fees

Joe Duran has strong opinions about how advisors should charge fees, especially given his outlook that planning is the value-add of the future. Duran urges advisors to charge for what the client truly values. "Too many advisors charge for investing, but give away planning. Yet they add no alpha to the client in investing, and they add tremendous value in financial guidance," he says. "As technology commoditizes investing, advisors will need to charge for how they really deliver value to clients in order to maintain client loyalty and profitability."

Despite the value financial planning can provide, many advisors are far too comfortable charging for investment management because that is what they know best. It seems as if the debate over the death of the AUM fee has been ongoing for well over a decade, and Chip Roame, for one, believes the familiar fee isn't going away anytime soon. "There's a lot of inertia to it. There are too many people paying that way to believe that, in the short run, there will be any material change to it," he said.

Regardless of whether you believe hard-dollar fees or AUM fees are the way of the future, one thing is for sure: Firms that put planning at the center of their value propositions need to ensure their service offerings justify a recurring fee. As AUM fees decline on the investment-management side, most firms that are forced to shift into a fee-for-service model have significantly harmed the valuation and cash flow of their practices. Also, as we have mentioned, clients need real-time financial management, and the fee to provide this service on a recurring basis isn't only good business; it's good for the client.

Mark Rutland wrote a blog post about the demise of Oldsmobile, and the story might be a lesson for advisors:

> The demise of Oldsmobile is a textbook example of a
> company getting ahead of itself and changing its message

before it had a new market to align with the new message. Management at Oldsmobile realized that it had a specific market that wanted a specific kind of car. For decades they had been convinced that there would always be people who wanted Oldsmobiles, and that those people would always want Oldsmobiles to look like Oldsmobiles. They did quite well with that market. The problem was that they were securing a growing share of a shrinking market. The people who wanted Oldsmobiles were elderly, and they were dying. Young people didn't want Oldsmobiles.

Seeing the handwriting on the wall, Oldsmobile hired an advertising agency to create a last-gasp, Hail Mary campaign to try to reach the younger car buyers who could give new life to the brand. The ad agency came up with quite a memorable slogan: This is not your father's Oldsmobile. It turned out to be the nail in the coffin for the Oldsmobile brand.[5]

With this cautionary tale in mind, we are reluctant to declare that the model we are espousing *is not your father's financial planning.*

Throughout this book, we've stressed that investment management will not set advisors apart from robos. Financial planning, coaching, and deeper relationships will be the value proposition of the future. As we have said before, this will be sophisticated financial planning, not the one-and-done plans that are presented to many clients. The advisor must be providing goals-based planning on an ongoing basis to justify the fee.

Recurring fees may be a hard sell to some clients and prospects. They pay their attorneys for an estate plan and don't pay the lawyer again until additional services are needed. It is very possible that advisors will get strong pushback from clients and prospects who object to that fee structure. The vast majority of clients and prospects will not decide to accept this arrangement overnight. They will wait until they get to know the advisor. It might take years for a client to realize that financial planning is worth paying for on a recurring basis. Many people need a catalyst to force them to initiate change. Recurring financial

---

[5] Dr. Mark Rutland, "'Not Your Father's Oldsmobile'—A Cautionary Tale," May 21, 2014, http://globalservants.org/connect/blog/165-not-your-fathers-oldsmobile.

planning can be an instrument of change for clients and their families. We believe as this story plays out, good advisors will be advisors not just on matters of finances, but also in matters of life. Families will be willing to pay ongoing fees for that in whatever form the best advisors choose to bill it.

Calling Foul on the Split of Assets

For a client and advisor relationship to become essential, both sides need to be reasonable and fair to each other. The splitting of assets happens today, but the digital advice platforms may cause it to occur more often. The splitting of assets happens when clients park some of their assets at a place like Vanguard and leave a portion of their portfolio at the advisor. For example, a client with $10 million in AUM may put $7 million outside the advisor's firm. It's unreasonable for an investor to expect $10 million worth of service when the advisor is only billing on $3 million. An investor cannot expect an advisor to act as a personal chief financial officer without paying enough fees to justify that level of service. However, this happens all the time and advisors we see accept it because that's easier than having a difficult discussion with the client or prospect. Advisors need to feel comfortable addressing this conflict directly and establishing a fee structure that is fair for the services provided. Use the pillars of value to make your case.

The Reversion . . . Good and Bad

While many financial advisors target high-net-worth clients, middle-income consumers are not as desirable to some firms. Some advisors find it difficult to service these kinds of accounts profitably. In most cases, advisors realize their usual hourly rates are not affordable for the middle-income client. Furthermore, if the client's assets are modest, charging a fee based on AUM will not be economically feasible for the advisor.

It will be interesting to see what happens to these middle-income prospects and how the services available to them will evolve over the next several years. As the robo advisors came on the scene, many medium-sized firms saw technology as a way to more effectively serve smaller accounts. The digital technology has created a great democratization of the industry, with more firms willing to take on clients who were not served in the past. As the digital platforms mature and larger financial institutions like Charles Schwab put massive amounts of money into advertising their intelligent portfolios, smaller and medium-sized firms might have to move back upstream to compete. Your average middle-sized firm or practice will not have the advertising capabilities to compete against Schwab and Vanguard for $250,000 accounts. What once seemed to promise an industry revolution will fizzle, causing the advisor model to revert to its old ways. Unless they are extremely large, firms trying to serve the middle-income client—a goal we believe is admirable—need to be careful in the way they create their service menu.

Ric Edelman, for example, doesn't segment. His $5,000 client gets the same advisor as his larger clients. Edelman has the advantage of having a large organization and more resources at his disposal. Firms with more limited resources are going to need to ensure they aren't providing the same service menu to someone with $5,000 under management as someone with $5 million. It's not unethical; it's business. We've seen firms set up separate entities and brands to serve different client segments while protecting against scope creep. This makes it much simpler to differentiate the fees.

DELIVERING ON YOUR VALUE PROPOSITION NEVER ENDS

Lululemon is still attempting to regain customer trust after the 2013 recall of the company's $98 yoga pants. The high-end pants became sheer when the person wearing them bent over, which was certainly a major problem for people assuming various yoga positions. Consumers who once relied on the brand to provide high-quality workout clothing, began to question if Lululemon was worth the price. Chipotle's value proposition is offering consumers large portions of fresh, locally sourced food, which is made to order while the customer watches. In 2015 many of its customers began to doubt the brand's safety when outbreaks of E. coli, salmonella, and norovirus caused serious health problems at a number of locations across the country.

No matter what price is charged for yoga pants or a burrito, consumers are unlikely to patronize any company that does not deliver on its value proposition. Similarly, it is pointless to ask what clients will pay for the services of a financial advisor who fails to deliver on the firm's value proposition. Many experts have predicted that the robo advisor movement will lead to fee compression for human advisors. If an advisor's value proposition is viewed favorably by clients, however, clients will be willing to pay more than they would for a robo advisor. In fact, they might be willing to pay higher fees than they do now. Ric Edelman told us, "Fee compression is not happening because of robos. Fee compression occurs at firms that have not provided value to consumers. The advisors that are seeing fee compression should look at themselves in the mirror because they're not providing value."

ESSENTIAL ADVISOR PRINCIPLE NO. 9
The Essential Advisor puts the investor's goals first and foremost—and the client notices.

If advisors deliver on their value propositions, they can take pride in having performed a valuable service in exchange for a fair and reasonable fee. Ideally, clients will describe their advisors with a variation of the Smith Barney tagline we discussed in Chapter 1: *"Our advisor makes money the old-fashioned way: She earns it."* The bottom line for advisors is they do not need to lower their fees. They should focus instead on making certain clients understand the fees they are paying and what they receive in return. The topic of fees should not be deflating; it should be a meaningful way to build stronger relationships. *Remember, in a world where people pay $5 for a cup of coffee, how much more will they pay for someone who changes their lives?*

THE CONSUMER PERSPECTIVE

Jason Zweig wrote an intriguing article for the *Wall Street Journal* entitled, "Why You're Paying Too Much in Fees." In the article, a financial advisor told a story about meeting with a prospective client. The advisor asked the prospect how much he was paying to

(Continued)

(*Continued*)

his advisory firm. The prospect said it was roughly $7,000 or $8,000. As it turned out, the client was paying 1.5 percent of $5 million, which equals $75,000.[6]

While this may be an uncommon occurrence, it's amazing to hear that consumers with $5 million invested haven't done the math to figure out how much they are paying in fees. Advisors should expect a very nasty phone call when it finally dawns on clients like this one that they are paying ten times what they thought. Since most advisors say their fees are negotiable, this client might consider asking to pay a lower percentage of AUM and paying separately for specific services.

More consumers will be having conversations like these as they become aware that it's up to them to educate themselves and protect their nest eggs. Consumers have come to realize they can't depend on securities regulators to protect them.

The point of this story is not to argue that consumers are better off with robo advisors who only charge a relatively small percentage of AUM. Unless the world changes dramatically and we're flying to our jobs with our jet packs, consumers will always prefer the human touch. Consumers are willing to pay more to deal with a person. While $75,000 seems to be a lot to pay for advisory services, it's a drop in the bucket if it protects the consumer from making emotional and irrational choices with his money. There's an old joke that asks: *How can I have a million-dollar stock portfolio? Start with $2 million.* It isn't hard for consumers to lose half their money, especially in view of the events that occurred in 2007 through 2009.

Consumers Are Learning What They Want

Surveys reveal consumers want a holistic approach. How big is the demand for this personal level of attention that goes beyond portfolio construction? Ask the Certified Financial Planner (CFP) board, and they say 66 percent., Pam Krueger would give the same estimate.

Aside from investors in favor of a holistic approach, 15 to 20 percent of investors are out there shopping for money managers based solely on performance. These consumers are willing to hand over their life savings with the expectation that the advisor will deliver alpha. These are the typical *Barron's* subscribers; they are not touchy-feely. They desire very little personal attention and hardly any real interaction. They will hire an advisor but won't get too attached. They'll fire an advisor in a heartbeat if their expectations are not met. The majority are men, and they fall squarely within the PBS *MoneyTrack* audience.

---

[6] Jason Zweig, "Why You're Paying Too Much in Fees," *Wall Street Journal,* June 19, 2016, http://blogs.wsj.com/moneybeat/2015/06/19/why-youre-paying-too-much-in-fees/.

The third group of investors is comprised of the 20 percent of consumers who truly do it all themselves because they like to be in charge. They jam their own strawberries and shear their own sheep and, when it comes to their money, they are their own experts.

Prospective clients are likely to be more anxious about fee discussions than an advisor is. The goal is for clients to feel that the fees they are paying are fair, reasonable, and commensurate with the value provided by an advisor. With many of the services people pay for, they're in a bind and have no choice but to accept the terms. Toilets leak, garage doors get stuck, and air conditioners break when it's 100 degrees outside. The big difference with financial services is that when advisors discuss fees, the prospective clients may not be as desperate to sign on the dotted line. Household repairs tend to be one-shot deals. If customers do not like the price or service, they aren't stuck with it for the long term. The next time something breaks, they'll call someone else.

Financial consumers need to become more knowledgeable buyers. Once that happens, many will be willing to pay for better advice because they will understand the benefits that come from that investment. Savvier buyers will also have clear expectations for advisors. They won't pay for a financial plan that is updated only once every three years, for example. Similarly, they are not going to pay significant amounts of money for advisory services, human or robo, that simply allocate their portfolio to passive funds.

Consumers should expect fee transparency so they're not caught by surprise when the bill comes. Everyone has been at the rental-car counter, bowled over by the total amount owed once taxes and fees nearly double the base rental price. It's not the rental car company's fault, but customers are not happy with the end result. When people stay at a hotel, they're probably ready for taxes, but are sometimes surprised by other charges such as resort and parking fees. The consumer financial experience shouldn't pose the same traps. Advisors need to be sure their clients know what kinds of fees and other expenses to expect. This information has to be concrete and specific, not a general overview, and advisors need to be proactive in addressing these issues instead of expecting clients to pore through the disclosure statements. When advisors are not forthcoming about fees, client satisfaction is likely to suffer. Consumers may conclude that the advisor might be hiding other material facts as well.

Smart consumers are becoming increasingly aware of the impact of fees on the long-term growth of their nest eggs. When an advisor emphasizes the firm's returns before advisory fees are deducted, a smart consumer will question the numbers. As discussed in Chapter 2, it isn't difficult for a consumer to use the Rule of 72 to challenge the advisor's projections.

How the Conversation Unfolds

Pam Krueger, was featured in an article about how to assess advisors, so a reader reached out to ask her for advice about what consumer should look for when selecting an advisor. The reader's profile was not unusual. He was an extremely educated and successful male in his forties—a demographic that will grow in the future. He was struggling to determine what he needed in terms of financial advice. A robo advisor seemed appealing based on cost, but something seemed to be missing. He had a couple of million dollars in a robo-only model, but didn't feel comfortable because he just "didn't know what he didn't know." He felt that if he could just find someone who would do complete a financial check from time to time, almost like a health physical, he would sleep better at night, but he wasn't aware if any advisors would perform that service.

Krueger put him through the WealthRamp process (www.wealthramp.com) to match him with an advisor who was willing to sit down and talk. The consumer described his conversation with the advisor as "outstanding." He and the advisor had an honest conversation about what he wanted and needed and what the advisor was able to provide. The key to the conversation was that the advisor was transparent that he needed to be paid for the value he would provide because the AUM fees for the small amount of money he would manage wouldn't cover his costs if the consumer kept the bulk of his assets in the robo advisor platform. The thing that impressed the consumer the most was "the transparency around fees . . . the advisor talked to me so openly about fees and the value he provided, it felt like a cold-case detective couldn't have paid more attention to detail." The advisor won a great new client, all based on true, open dialogue about what matters.

KEY TAKEAWAYS

- Transparency in fees is a big selling point for digital advice platforms. As their message gets to a wider audience, advisors will need to get comfortable talking about fees with clients.
- Digital advice providers are confusing the consumer because they focus the discussion on cost instead of value. Sometimes, they are the same thing, but in most cases, they aren't. Consumers and advisors need to be clear about what costs are being paid for what menu of services. To borrow an analogy from the automotive industry, you wouldn't expect to pay the same amount for a Ferrari as you would for a Honda Accord.

- The Essential Advisors, along with the best consumers, will not fear the fee discussion, but relish it as an opportunity to deepen relationships and clarify expectations.

- The fee discussion should start at the beginning of a relationship. Advisors should conduct a needs analysis to see what services their clients want. Advisors may think they are adding value by offering a particular service, but it might not be important to the client. There is often a disconnect between what advisors think their clients want and what they actually want, and this can lead to fee issues down the road.

- If investors do not understand what fees they are paying, they are less likely to trust an advisor. It is also less likely they will refer friends, relatives, and business associates to the advisor.

CHAPTER 9

Finding the Essential Advisor

Excellence is never an accident. It is always the result of high intention, sincere effort, and int elligent execution; it represents the wise choice of many alternatives—choice, not chance, determines your destiny.

—Aristotle

For those consumers who haven't yet cut the cord on cable, the entire television experience is somewhat baffling. As Bill often jokes, "I don't watch much television, but when I do, it would be nice to have something on that I actually enjoy. It's amazing that with over 200 channels there never seems to be anything on that's good." Once consumers decide they need financial help, they may face a similar dilemma: *There are thousands of advisors, but how do I find the right one?* The journey to articulate and understand value for both advisors and clients succeeds only if they know how to find one another.

Let's face it, consumers are not going to find the right advisor by conducting a search on Google. When consumers plug in the phrase "financial advice" into a search engine, they will get over seven million hits. Hopefully, they won't settle for an advisor who knows more about search engine optimization than financial planning.

A GROWING NUMBER OF CHOICES

The rise of the digital marketplace is going to bring even more choices to consumers with small and medium-sized investment portfolios. Banks are going to have better digital offerings. Mutual fund companies and asset managers who used to focus only on selling products to end consumers will offer comprehensive advice platforms. It is good for consumers to have choices, but the sheer volume of options may be overwhelming. Don't allow the perception of this selection process to be so daunting that, as a consumer, you become paralyzed. Advisors shouldn't worry about reaching end consumers. The reality is good advisors will always grow—not at a rate like Google or Apple, but your firm or practice can grow if you make yourself essential to your clients.

In Search of the Right Advisor

The search for the right financial advisor can be difficult. Obviously, credentials and experience help to separate one advisor from another. Unrealistic assurances from an advisor should be a prospect's cue to walk away. It's old advice, but it still holds water: If something sounds too good to be true, it probably is. In the financial advisory industry, value propositions might sound too good to be true, so consumers need to be very careful when selecting an advisor. The Internet makes it a whole lot easier to conduct due diligence on a financial advisor. It helps to start with recommendations from relatives and business associates. A consumer's due diligence should not stop there, however.

The decision to hire a financial advisor should not be based on reputation alone. After all, investors swore by Bernie Madoff until they learned he had operated a Ponzi scheme and had perpetrated one of the largest financial frauds in U.S. history.

Advisor Matchmaking in the Digital Era

Pam Krueger has added enormously to our understanding of how consumers view advisors. Pam is the founder of the *MoneyTrack* program, which appears on hundreds of public television stations across the country. She recently launched WealthRamp, a service that helps people, especially women, find qualified financial advisors. Pam has observed that finding the best financial advisor is usually a very stressful search for most people. Many consumers are confused by advisors' credentials and do not know how to ask the right questions. Most consumers value their privacy and dislike discussing how much money they have with someone they barely know.

The right advisor can make that situation less stressful. If the relationship is a good fit, it will be easy for the person to open up to the advisor. Pam believes that WealthRamp is the equivalent of a matchmaking service for consumers and advisors. It helps consumers to make a rational choice when faced with a list of advisors. Just as there are many qualities people seek in a spouse or business partner, there are many qualities an advisor should have. The challenge for consumers is finding a compatible and competent advisor. More and more platforms like WealthRamp will likely appear in the future with the goal of using behavioral science to match consumers and advisors.

THE ESSENTIAL ADVISOR

If you've been paying attention, throughout the last five chapters we've been laying out what we believe are the principles of the Essential Advisor. We believe these principles serve as a great way for consumers and advisors to discuss whether or not they are a good fit. Before you even comparing advisors, how do you know what you are looking for? Here are all the principles in one place and the discussion points we believe should lead to the right start of a relationship.

The Essential Advisor:

- Clearly identifies his or her expertise and works with investors whose needs are closely aligned.
    - The consumers should understand what services and client types make up the bulk of the practice. If the advisor services mostly corporate executives and you are the owner of a small flower shop, it might be worth discussing the fit.
    - The wrong fit doesn't do anybody any good. Advisors feel like they are spending too much time for what they're being

paid, and consumers end up feeling like they are paying for a lack of value.

- Puts the investor's goals first and foremost.

  - There are Essential Advisors in all forms of financial distribution. There are conflicts in the wirehouse (brokerage) model, but there are great advisors there. There are great advisors in registered investment advisors (RIAs), banks, and independent broker-dealers. Consumers should ask the question: Can you give me an example where your business model might get in the way of putting my interests first? How did you overcome that in the past? No matter what the model, good advisors will have a true and honest answer.

- Helps investors cut through the noise.

  - The consumer should ask the advisor how they keep their clients focused on what really matters.

- Works to understand each client's personal circumstances, values, investing style, tax situation, and goals.

  - Hopefully this is something the consumer gets a feel for quickly as part of the financial planning process with the advisor. If that doesn't happen early on, the consumer should ask the advisor how they help support goals and determine financial and other priorities.

- Develops and carefully monitors a personal plan for each client and makes timely portfolio adjustments to meet changing circumstances and needs.

  - The consumer doesn't need to understand everything about the investment philosophies of the advisor, but some key questions are: Do you believe in changing portfolios significantly? When you do, does it impact the fees I pay or the revenue you generate?

- Receives the first call when a client is faced with a life transition, responding with true care and concern.

  - The consumer should understand if they want this type of relationship before they sit down with a potential advisor. If they just want an investment manager, this type of discussion shouldn't be on the table.

- If the consumer decides they want this type of relationship they should ask questions like: When my spouse unexpectedly passed away, can you walk me through how you assisted? If I'm considering long-term-care insurance, how would you help me assess that decision?

- Helps the investor understand fees and expenses—and the value provided for those dollars.

  - The consumer should understand how costs are managed—and the key question, depending on tax bracket is: how do you help me manage taxes?

  - As we discussed in Chapter 8, advisors and consumers who can't talk about fees won't build a relationship.

- Tailors communication, education, and the overall client experience to meet the unique needs, style, and concerns of each client.

  - The consumer should be clear on a few things before they sit down with an advisor: How much are they willing to delegate? Do they expect the advisor to educate them on financial issues or do they not care? How often do they want to be communicated with and how do they want to be communicated with (phone, e-mail, etc.)?

  - Once the consumer has clear preferences on the above items, the advisor and consumer should have a discussion around the client experience and how it can be catered to meet these needs.

- Communicates clearly, truthfully, and consistently: enough said on that one.

- Effectively utilizes technology to maximize the time spent with clients.

  - A consumer should feel very comfortable asking an advisor how they spend their day. How much time with clients, employees, and others in the field? If an advisor is spending less than 50 percent of their time with clients, that should be a red flag.

Knowing what it takes to be essential to a client is important for an advisor to build their practice around as well as a great framework for the consumer to assess the advisor. There are also some other obvious questions that need to be discussed and some deeper questions we would recommend.

The Obvious Questions

1. How long have you been in the industry?
2. Where did you study to get your degree?
3. How many firms have you been with or is this your only one?
4. Why did you choose to affiliate with or start this firm or practice?
5. How many people work with you in the servicing of clients?

Other Key Questions

1. Do you have a succession plan? Explain what would happen if something happened to you?
2. Why do you enjoy doing what you do?
3. Do you work in teams or on your own?
4. What has your employee and client turnover been like in the last three years?
5. The last three clients that left . . . why did they leave?
6. Do you have other family members working in the business?

AVOIDING THE BAIT AND SWITCH

The bait and switch may be an intentional scheme to get a consumer's business then change the terms, but oftentimes it's not. It can happen when a prospect gets very close to the onboarding advisor and then over time sees that person less and less, only to be working with someone new. The best advisors work in teams. There are certainly going to be different personnel involved in the relationship. Clients shouldn't want their advisors to be focused on taking calls to transfer money or filling out paperwork, as there are better uses of their time. Some firms will have sales-focused individuals who bring clients in, then shift the account to relationship managers. Usually this will be clear up front, but consumers should ask if the people they are working with in the onboarding will be their team going forward.

With good advisors, the bait and switch usually happens unintentionally. Good advisors are in high demand, whether they run their own practices or sit inside an institution. Not considering life events, the first two years of a new relationship is extremely time consuming. The advisor needs to spend a lot of time with new clients, as the financial planning process is time intensive. During this period both sides can truly get to know each other and get comfortable in their relationship and the process. After the first couple of years, the relationship requires less time to be spent together—not because the advisor no longer cares, but because there's less discovery and work to be done because the major decisions have likely been made. For firms that are growing, it's easy for the advisor to be so focused on the newer relationships than the older ones that are more on cruise control. Advisors need to be mindful of this balance and if teammates need to change to serve the needs of the client, it should be articulated clearly and in a transparent way.

We've heard way too many stories from consumers who grew really fond of working with a particular advisor, only to have their long-term relationship managed by someone else, without a discussion. In most cases the consumer will be equally happy, but the transition needs to be handled well. Consumers should ask about this up front and be clear about their expectations on this topic.

IT'S OKAY TO SAY NO

Although we are offering views from the consumer's perspective, we believe that advisors should be fairly compensated. We also believe that some clients expect too much service, performance, and attention for the fees they are paying. These clients aren't going to be happy unless the advisor's investment strategies produce enough returns to pay for whatever they want to buy. Some of them want to live like the Kardashians—without the Kardashians' money.

We all know people who are high maintenance, and every minor glitch in life results in high drama. These types of clients will never be satisfied with an advisor, his accountant, or the other professionals they deal with in the course of a day. We don't blame advisors who try to avoid clients who will take up too much of their time. They come to realize that these clients will never be satisfied, no matter how much value the advisor brings to the relationship. Whether it's in an advisory relationship or the local grocery store, there are some clients and customers who are not worth having. If you ever stood behind someone with a shopping cart full of groceries in the 10-item express line, you'll share our belief that the customer isn't always right.

Sometimes advisors are their own worst enemy and raise clients' expectations too high in their advertisements and marketing materials. The goal of advisors should be to meet and exceed their clients' expectations, not to disappoint them. Aside from that problem, advisors should be careful because regulators frown on promissory statements in advertisements and language that might be construed as a guarantee.

THE ADVISOR OF THE FUTURE

Jay's circle of friends consists of young and very bright people who are not in the financial services field. They ask him incredibly perceptive questions about robo advisors, fee transparency, and the value of advice. Keep in mind that these are not people who read about these topics for a living. They have heard about them in the course of their daily lives. When Jay explains the value of advice, they get it.

The consumer of the future who right now is 35 to 45 years old, will have much more money in 10 years, and will be the perfect client for advisors. These consumers will be well educated and sophisticated about what advisors can do for them. That environment will be amenable for good advisors.

If we were hiring the advisor of the future, the person would look more like a coach and would possess a very broad skill set in life-event planning. The individual would be someone who studied psychology (or another behavioral science), as well as finance. Few educational programs exist today with that overlapping curriculum, but we hope more pop up as these overlapping skills will serve clients better in the future. The advisor of the future must be more than just a numbers person, since the value proposition goes well beyond being able to crunch the numbers for a client. The person must understand the emotional issues clients face. Without empathy and interpersonal skills, advisors will be of no use as they counsel clients during life transitions. In an ironic twist, it appears as if we are saying advisors of the future need to behave differently or be trained differently, but this is more a comment of scale—more great advisors need to be educated and trained. The great advisors over the past 20 years and today are already doing what we ascribe for the future.

We've said before that coaching and counseling can be an important element of an advisor's value proposition. When the Dow Jones Industrial Average drops 500 points or more in a day, some clients are badly in need of counseling and therapy. We believe only humans have the capacity to provide those services.

A FINAL STORY

In a memorable episode of *The West Wing*, the president's chief of staff, Leo McGarry, talks with his deputy, Josh Lyman, who is suffering from posttraumatic stress syndrome after being wounded in an assassination attempt. McGarry tells Lyman this story:

> This guy's walking down a street when he falls in a hole. The walls are so steep, he can't get out. A doctor passes by, and the guy shouts up, "Hey you, can you help me out?" The doctor writes a prescription, throws it down in the hole and moves on. Then a priest comes along, and the guy shouts up "Father, I'm down in this hole, can you help me out?" The priest writes out a prayer, throws it down in the hole and moves on. Then a friend walks by. "Hey Joe, it's me, can you help me out?" And the friend jumps in the hole. Our guy says, "Are you stupid? Now we're both down here." The friend says, "Yeah, but I've been down here before, and I know the way out."

When financial advisors help to guide their clients through life transitions, they offer guidance from the perspective of someone who has been in that hole helping others. Advisors know their way out of whatever financial hole clients find themselves in, no matter if the clients were pushed over the edge or wielded the shovel. Maybe the advisor hasn't lost a spouse, but he or she has counseled people who have. In our opinion, you'll never get that help from a robo advisor, no matter how many advances in artificial intelligence there are. Only humans have the emotional temperament to guide clients in their time of need, whether it's the dissolution of a marriage or helping a grandparent help a grandchild with college expenses. In contrast, a robo advisor might spit out the equivalent of a prescription or prayer, not empathy and compassion.

The best financial advisors can help clients through all of those transitions. And when they provide real value to one client, that person will sing their praises to the next person who falls in that same dark hole and needs help getting out.

In time, a financial advisor can become the go-to person for current and prospective clients who need assistance with the life transitions that may await all of us. When advisors establish their value transition in a community, they can come to be known as a resource for people who find themselves in the same predicament. In some small way, they can become the person everyone listens to, like what E. F. Hutton claimed to be. No, it won't be like the commercial we referenced in Chapter 1 where people around the pool stop when the advisor's name is mentioned. Nevertheless, an advisor's value proposition can be an equally effective marketing tool. More people should be reaching out and getting advice.

The best advisors take the emotion out of money. They filter out the noise and help their clients avoid being deluged by information.

As Warren Buffett has said on many occasions, successful investing takes time, discipline, and patience. By adhering to a well-designed plan, investors can stay on course. They need to ignore the market commentators who are screeching at them from their television sets. For the most part, it is all noise that can cause investors to panic.

You won't see a consumer perspective to end this chapter because we believe this entire chapter has had a consumer angle. Our journey together stops here. Please see the outstanding "Last Word" written by our friend Jud Bergman, one of the financial technology industry's most respected chief executives.

The predictions outlined in this book will not happen overnight. We believe this full evolution of the industry may take a decade or more to fully materialize, but the rate of change continues to pick up. Hopefully, this book will still be in print, or you'll keep a copy in your office, and you can see if we were more right or wrong.

The one thing we know for sure is that people will always need advice to reach their goals and to confidently meet the challenges of life. We believe the institutions or advisors delivering this advice will forever be *essential*.

The Last Word

I am thrilled to collaborate with Bill and Jay in the development of this book and the principles that guide it. Each of us believe in the power of sound financial advice and we understand it is needed more now than ever. Wealth management as a profession is at an inflection. Will developing technology disrupt the best advisors' practices or strengthen them? To some, this inflection point will be painful. But for advisors who embrace the transformative opportunity, the best days as wealth advisors are yet to unfold.

I remember growing up in Minnesota and my father taking our family to Summit Avenue in Saint Paul, a mansioned boulevard on a bluff overlooking the Mississippi. The avenue is a crystallization from another time. Here, F. Scott Fitzgerald lived—on the side away from the river views—in a row house. Imagining how the "other" side of the avenue might have looked through the eyes of the young author, it's not hard to see elements of the tycoon's mansion and grounds that he later drew on for his masterwork, *The Great Gatsby.*

On Summit Avenue there was one mansion that stood out. It was built by James J. Hill, a Canadian immigrant and founder of the Great Northern Railway, which connected the Twin Cities of Minneapolis and Saint Paul to the Pacific Ocean. The railway became the northernmost transcontinental route in the United States, and of note the only privately funded—and successfully built—transcontinental railroad in American history.

Hill's personal fortune was estimated to be more than $60 million at the time of his death in 1916, the equivalent of $1.4 billion in today's dollars. My father, a businessman and former history instructor, explained to our family that most people believed Hill's great accomplishment was building a transcontinental railroad, which explains the nickname he came to be known by: the Empire Builder (which, to this day identifies in his honor the Amtrak train that runs from Chicago to Seattle). But my father saw it differently. Hill's achievement was more about the connections the railroad enabled. Hill connected farmers and their produce from Minnesota's Red River Valley and the Dakotas with millers like General Mills and Pillsbury, brewers and distillers; lumber from the North Woods with big-city builders; iron ore producers from the Mesabi Range with steelmakers back east; ranchers' cattle with meat-packers, unleashing the potential of a huge inland "empire."

Wealth management today resembles the railroad system as Hill envisioned it. Digital technologies are the "steel rails" that form the backbone for much of what we do, but the connections among participants in our industry—the advisors, broker-dealers, insurers, bankers, home offices, investment managers, strategists, and custodians—has become much more than just a digital network. It's a dynamic ecosystem that affords powerful leverage for those best able to take full advantage of its connections and resources. To unleash its full potential, participants in the network must create deeper engagement—both personal and digital—with their investors, helping their clients find the best routes to meeting their goals. By doing this, advisors can provide significantly more value than any digital advice provider alone ever could.

UNLOCKING THE VALUE OF THE INDEPENDENT ADVISOR

In his autobiography, on the very first page as I remember it, Hill writes: "The most fortunate of individuals have in their life one great adventure—this railroad has been mine."

Many of you reading this book are also on a "great adventure": the adventure of building a business or, a wealth management practice, which is as much about making connections as was Hill's railroad. Until relatively recently, many independent advisors were like the early pioneers of the Red River Valley—self-reliant because they had to be, but removed from the productivity benefits of a network. The fertile farmland spanning northwest Minnesota, northeast North Dakota, and southern Manitoba was accessible only by boat, and even then for only part of the year. The area's residents had no timely way to get supplies they needed to farm the fertile soil, or to deliver crops to market. Then came more powerful enabling technology and prosperity was the result for the participants. Advisors are at their best when they can efficiently leverage a vast community network of resources that strengthens engagement with clients.

CROSSING THE DIGITAL DIVIDE

Yet, even as Hill's railroad helped to dramatically expand trade, commerce, and culture in the upper Midwest and northern Great Plains, his vision endured that he would connect these communities by rail with the Pacific Northwest. But he had a problem: the Rocky Mountains, the Continental Divide, and the capital it would take to bridge it. Hill sought to connect the Twin Cities with the Pacific Ocean through the straightest and shortest route possible. Conventional wisdom said that the only way to cross the Continental Divide was to bore tunnels under the Rocky Mountains, but Hill found a better way. He famously said that he did not care enough for Rocky Mountain scenery to spend a large amount of money settling it. His focus was efficiency—the shortest distance, the lowest grade and the least amount of expenditure. Hill had a different approach.

Native Americans had long described a traversable gap in the Rockies that had eluded white explorers. Yet, in December 1889, aided by a Flathead Indian guide, Hill's chief engineer, John Stevens (a fearless Maine native who later was chief engineer on the Panama Canal project) walked the Marias Pass in Montana—in 40-below weather! What Lewis and Clark and countless others had tried, Stevens and Hill had accomplished. The Marias Pass, the lowest crossing of the Rocky Mountains, allowed the Great Northern to expand through the Rockies without boring a tunnel. In 1890, Stevens crossed another pass—now called Stevens Pass—in Washington's Cascade Mountains. When the final spike in the Great Northern Railway was laid in 1893, Hill had accomplished what few thought was possible without government subsidy. He had traversed the Rocky Mountains, connecting the Pacific Northwest, the Upper Midwest, and the Great Plains to the rest of the country.

I believe that many and perhaps even most advisors today have a Digital Divide that separates their practices from a more complete engagement with their clients. This Divide exists between those who have fully embraced the benefits of technology and advisors who have not; those who have systematized and automated the lowest-value areas of their practices and those who have not; those who are able to share these benefits directly with their clients, and those who cannot.

Here's an example: many advisors with whom I interact still don't have a powerful client portal. Over the years, I've asked many why not. The response I hear most often is, "My clients don't want it. They rely on me to meet with them and show them how they're doing." These advisors are stuck on the Eastern side of the Rockies, having yet to cross the Digital Divide. Crossing the Digital Divide is essential for advisors to leverage their core strengths, build deeper connections with current clients and engage new ones, particularly tech-savvy Millennials. Those who do not cross the Digital Divide will face digital disruption at the hands of those that do cross it. Those who do cross the Divide successfully will deliver better outcomes for their clients, and experience increased productivity and expanded markets. Of course, these were the same benefits that accrued to the countless participants in Hill's railway network.

HERE WE GO AGAIN: IT'S MORE THAN MAN VERSUS MACHINE

One last thought. Many financial publications and advisors themselves seem to frame the promising advances in digital advice technology as a kind of "man versus machine" choice. Binary: one or the other, as if consumers are choosing between a human and a robot. But the reality is much more interesting.

Of course, this man versus machine concept isn't new. In 1996, Garry Kasparov, perhaps the greatest chess champion of all time, took on the IBM computer "Deep Blue" in a six-game chess match. Few believed Kasparov stood a chance. The headlines were simple: "Man versus Machine." Kasparov's brilliant and aggressive play enabled a 4–2 upset victory, despite the fact that Deep Blue was able to calculate 4 million scenarios per second.

The IBM team requested a rematch and Kasparov agreed. By the time of the 1997 rematch, Deep Blue could analyze 6 million positions per second. There was a fascinating moment in the rematch where Deep Blue timed out, and could not select a move that improved its position, and then defaulted to a meaningless move which did not surrender position, a sort of "throwaway" move that Kasparov could not make sense of. He wondered why the superior computing capacity of Deep Blue would make a nontactical move. As a result, Kasparov assumed the computer was smarter or creative in an unchartered way and was developing a strategy he had never seen before. As a result, he overreacted, and made a move which Deep Blue was then able to exploit. Of course, Kasparov could not have known Deep Blue had experienced a programming "glitch" of sorts. Deep Blue went on to win the match 3.5–2.5.

The headlines following the 1997 rematch read: "Man Loses to Machine." Kasparov pointed out the absurd oversimplification of the headlines: the "computer" which "won," was expertly operated by dozens of programmers who performed real-time optimization, based on Kasparov's latest positon. Deep Blue was the beneficiary of a human team with the ability to analyze in real time all the moves Kasparov had ever made in any match, as well as all the moves of many of the grand masters, and also potential optimized improvements, with each move. It wasn't Man versus Machine so much as it was: Dozens of Humans + Machine versus Garry Kasparov.

After retiring from competitive tournament chess, Kasparov excelled in a new form of chess: "advanced" chess, also known as "freestyle" chess, where players leverage computer programs in matches against other players, and also against supercomputers (without the benefit of real-time programmers for the supercomputer). Here's the interesting part: freestyle chess players have shown that good players (not grand master caliber), armed with basic PC-based software, can beat the most advanced computer-only programs. Why is this important? It reveals the true insight: human experts PLUS machines deliver better results than machines alone can.

Said differently, wealth management isn't going to be taken over by digital robots, but getting over the digital divide requires us to embrace technology. The winning strategy for our profession will look something like Kasparov's freestyle chess: smart advisors supported by great technology, creating an unbeatable experience where they leverage technology to drive down the cost of commoditized processes and spend more time with their clients.

The best days for advisors and their clients are yet to unfold. Bill and Jay's book lays out an excellent framework for winning in our digital age. Advisors who follow the principles outlined here and who are able to cross the Digital Divide to enrich and deepen their relationships with investors will deliver better outcomes for their clients, experience increased productivity, and enjoy expanded markets for their services.

The time is now for *The Essential Advisor.*

Jud Bergman
Chairman and CEO, Envestnet

About the Interviewees

JOSEPH J. DURAN, CEO, UNITED CAPITAL, CFA®

Joe Duran is chief executive officer and founding partner of United Capital, the nation's first and largest financial life management company. United Capital currently manages more than $15 billion in client assets and advises on $7 billion in plan assets. The firm has more than 70 locations and 600 employees.

Duran is a renowned industry visionary with featured columns in both *InvestmentNews* and Time Inc.'s Money.com. He is a frequent contributor to CNBC, Fox Business, Bloomberg, and PBS, and appears regularly in both traditional and online media. Duran is a recipient of a prestigious Ernst & Young Entrepreneur of the Year award in 2015 and the Schwab Pacesetter Impact award. His most recent book, *The Money Code: Improve Your Entire Financial Life Right Now*, achieved best-seller status on both the *New York Times* and *USA Today* lists. Most importantly, Duran is lucky to have a wonderful family who inspire him every day. He, his wife Jen, and their daughters Charlotte, Juliette, and Samantha live in Newport Coast, California.

RIC EDELMAN, CHAIRMAN AND CEO, EDELMAN FINANCIAL SERVICES

Edelman Financial Services was founded by chairman and CEO Ric Edelman, who was ranked three times as the number-one independent financial advisor in the nation by *Barron's*. In addition to providing financial advice for 28 years, Edelman also hosts a weekly radio show and a syndicated television show, both airing nationwide. He is also a number-one *New York Times* best-selling author who has published eight books on personal finance, winning multiple "book of the year" awards. His latest book, *The Truth About Retirement Plans and*

IRAs, is a number-one national bestseller. Edelman is an inductee of the Financial Advisor Hall of Fame, sponsored by *Research* magazine.

With 122 financial planners and 42 offices coast-to-coast, Edelman Financial Services manages more than $15 billion for more than 30,000 individuals and families and has won more than 100 business, advisory, communication, and community service awards. Visit Edelman online at RicEdelman.com (www.edelmanfinancial.com).

PATRICIA FARRAR-RIVAS, CEO, VERIS WEALTH PARTNERS

Patricia Farrar-Rivas is a founding principal and CEO of Veris Wealth Partners LLC. She has been providing investment advisory and wealth management services since 1992. Farrar-Rivas has co-led Veris's work with Envestnet Asset Management to deliver impact investment solutions to investment advisors. Prior to Veris, Farrar-Rivas led the effort by Silicon Valley–based public accounting firm Frank, Rimerman + Co. to launch its new investment advisory subsidiary, Frank, Rimerman Advisors. She also cofounded the New York office of Progressive Asset Management in 1994, the first socially responsible brokerage firm.

Farrar-Rivas is a member of the Standards Council for the Sustainability Accounting Standards Board (SASB). She has been a Certified Investment Management Analyst (CIMA®) since 2000 and is a Certified Investment Strategist (CIS). She is also a member of the Investment Management Consultants Association (IMCA). Farrar-Rivas is based in San Francisco, where she lives with her family.

ZACHARY KARABELL, HEAD OF GLOBAL STRATEGY, ENVESTNET

Zachary Karabell is head of global investment strategy for Envestnet. Karabell was previously executive vice president, head of marketing, and chief economist at Fred Alger Management, a New York–based investment firm.

Educated at Columbia, Oxford, and Harvard, where he received his PhD, Karabell is the author of more than a dozen books, including the recently published *The Leading Indicators: A Short History of the Numbers That Rule Our World* (Simon & Schuster, 2014) and *Superfusion:*

How China and America Became One Economy and Why the World's Prosperity Depends on It (Simon & Schuster, 2009) and previous books such as *The Last Campaign: How Harry Truman Won the 1948 Election* (which won the Chicago Tribune Heartland Prize for best nonfiction book of the year).

In 2003, the World Economic Forum designated Karabell a "Global Leader for Tomorrow." He is a regular commentator on national news programs, such as CNBC and CNN, and a contributor to such publications as *Politico*, the *Wall Street Journal*, the *Los Angeles Times*, the *New York Times*, *Time*, *Slate*, and *Foreign Affairs*.

MICHAEL E. KITCES, PARTNER AND DIRECTOR OF FINANCIAL PLANNING, PINNACLE ADVISORY GROUP

Michael E. Kitches is a partner and the director of financial planning for Pinnacle Advisory Group, a private wealth management firm located in Columbia, Maryland that oversees approximately $1.8 billion of client assets. In addition, he is a cofounder of the XY Planning Network (www.xyplanningnetwork.com) and New Planner Recruiting (www.newplannerrecruiting.com), the former Practitioner Editor of the *Journal of Financial Planning*, and the publisher of the popular financial planning industry blog *Nerd's Eye View* through his website Kitces.com, dedicated to advancing knowledge in financial planning. In 2010, Kitces was recognized with one of the FPA's "Heart of Financial Planning" awards for his dedication and work in advancing the profession.

VALERIE NEWELL, CHAIRMAN, RIVERPOINT CAPITAL MANAGEMENT

Valerie Newell is the chairman of RiverPoint Capital Management and director of the Private Client and High-Net-Worth Group. As a veteran of the investment management and financial services industry for more than 25 years, Newell has extensive financial expertise and experience. She was ranked #29 on *Barron's* 2015 List of Top 100 Independent Wealth Advisors and in 2011 was named as one of the Top Women Registered Investment Advisors in America. Newell has also been named a Five-Star Wealth Manager by *Cincinnati Magazine* every year since 2008.

Prior to joining RiverPoint in 2002, Newell was a managing director of Scudder, Stevens & Clark Private Investment Counsel and director of the Cincinnati Office. Scudder, prior to its purchase by Deutsche Bank, was a long-standing independent investment advisor with national and international operations.

SHIRL PENNEY, CHIEF EXECUTIVE OFFICER, DYNASTY FINANCIAL PARTNERS

Shirl Penney is the founder of Dynasty Financial Partners. Formerly he was director of business development for Global Wealth Advisory Services at Citi Smith Barney. Before that, he was head of executive financial services and director of private wealth management at Smith Barney. Under his tenure, his group was named High Net Worth Platform of the Year for 2002, 2003, 2005, and 2006 by *Private Asset Management* magazine. In 2015 Shirl was recognized by *InvestmentNews* magazine's 40 Under 40 as a leader in the financial services industry.

Penney received a BA in economics from Bates College. He serves as president of the Clarence E. Townsend Foundation, which supports various individuals and groups in need in his home state of Maine.

JIM PRATT-HEANEY, CHIEF INVESTMENT OFFICER, LLBH PRIVATE WEALTH MANAGEMENT

Jim Pratt-Heaney is a founding partner and chief investment officer of LLBH Private Wealth Management, with 30 years of experience in the financial services industry. Prior to LLBH, Jim held executive level positions across many investment firms such as EF Hutton, Smith Barney, and Merrill Lynch Private Banking and Investing Group. Pratt-Heaney has been named a 2015 Five Star Wealth and a Leading Wealth Advisor by *Worth* magazine. He is a contributing author to *Worth* magazine and other industry publications. He has also been featured on Fox Business Channel and the Dow Jones advisor show, and is frequently cited in local and national press.

Pratt-Heaney is a graduate of Marist College with continuing education at The Ohio State University and The Wharton School of Management Center. He lives in Weston, Connecticut, with his wife. When not working, Pratt-Heaney loves playing tennis, music, traveling, and spending time with his children and their growing families.

CHIP ROAME, MANAGING PARTNER, TIBURON STRATEGIC ADVISORS

Chip Roame is the managing partner of Tiburon Strategic Advisors, one of the financial industry's leading providers of research, strategy consulting, and other related services since 1998. Prior to founding Tiburon Strategic Advisors, Roame was a consultant with McKinsey & Company. He has served on the boards of a variety of start-up ventures and currently serves as a director of Envestnet. Roame received an MBA from the University of Michigan and a BA from Michigan State University.

KNUT A. ROSTAD, PRESIDENT, INSTITUTE FOR THE FIDUCIARY STANDARD

Knut A. Rostad, MBA cofounded and chaired the Committee for the Fiduciary Standard and cofounded and is president of the Institute for the Fiduciary Standard, a nonprofit formed in 2011 to advance the fiduciary standard through research, education and advocacy.

The Institute for the Fiduciary Standard seeks to advance fiduciary principles in investment advice. The Institute has established the Institute's Six Core Fiduciary Duties, the Fiduciary Declaration, Fiduciary September the Frankel Fiduciary Prize, and advocates for a true fiduciary standard before the SEC and DOL. Rostad was named to *Investment Adviser* magazine's "IA 25" list in 2014, which it calls "our annual list of the most influential people in and around the advisor industry."

Rostad earned a BA in political science at the University of Vermont and an MBA from the Norwegian School of Management. He is an Accredited Investment Fiduciary (AIF®) with the Center for Fiduciary Studies, Pittsburgh.

BILL SCHIFFMAN, PRESIDENT AND COFOUNDER OF SCHIFFMAN, GROW & CO. AND SG FINANCIAL SERVICES, LLC

Bill Schiffman often says (tongue in cheek) that "he has more licenses than sense." In addition to being a certified public accountant, he holds Series 7 and 66 qualifications, and has life, health, and annuity insurance licenses. Aside from allowing him the joy of countless hours of continuing education, this combination of achieved standards allows Schiffman to provide a complete array of experienced consulting acumen to his clients. He has an extremely strong relationship with his broker-dealer, Valmark Securities, Inc.

Schiffman is married to Lynne Aronson, and they have multiple four-legged children. He has been the host of WOSU-TV's high school quiz program "In The Know" for 33 years. In what little free time he has, Bill enjoys travel, cooking, reading unpopular literature, charitable work, and almost all sports. His greatest passion aside from family and business is thoroughbred horse racing, and he is involved in several racing/breeding ownership ventures.

MARK TIBERGIEN, CHIEF EXECUTIVE OFFICER, PERSHING ADVISOR SOLUTIONS

Mark Tibergien is chief executive officer of Pershing Advisor Solutions, a BNY Mellon company. Pershing Advisor Solutions is one of the country's leading custodians for registered investment advisors and family offices. Prior to joining Pershing, Tibergien was principal at the accounting and consulting firm, Moss Adams LLP, where he was partner-in-charge of the Business Consulting group, chairman of the Financial Services Industry group, and partner-in-charge of the Business Valuation Group.

Tibergien has worked with public and private companies on matters related to business management, transition planning and strategy formulation since 1976. He is the author of three books published by Bloomberg Press, *Practice Made Perfect*; *How to Value, Buy or Sell a Financial Advisory Practice*; and *Practice Made (More) Perfect*. He has also been a regular columnist for *Investor Advisor* magazine on management issues since 2005.

ELLIOT S. WEISSBLUTH, CHIEF EXECUTIVE OFFICER, HIGHTOWER

Elliot S. Weissbluth is founder and CEO of HighTower, a national financial services firm built by and for elite financial advisors. Weissbluth is frequently recognized as an influencer in the financial services industry. He has appeared on *Worth* magazine's Power 100 list, *Investment Advisor*'s list of the Top 25 Most Influential People, RIAbiz's list of Most Influential Figures in the RIA Business, and *InvestmentNews*' Power 20 list. He wrote the foreword to Tony Robbins' best-selling book *Money: Master the Game*.

Weissbluth is also a LinkedIn Influencer—a member of a prestigious group of thought leaders invited to share insights with the LinkedIn community on a monthly basis—and a regular guest on major broadcast networks, including CNBC, Fox Business, and Bloomberg. He sits on the boards of the Young Presidents' Organization (Chicago chapter) and Endeavor Global, a global nonprofit that transforms emerging countries by supporting high-impact entrepreneurs.

About the Authors

BILL CRAGER, PRESIDENT, ENVESTNET

Bill Crager is the president of Envestnet, which he cofounded in 1999. Crager has led the firm's platform, product, and marketing strategy as well as the company's relationship engagements. Along with Envestnet chairman and CEO Jud Bergman, he has been a driving force behind a firm that has in just 16 years become the leading managed solutions service provider in terms of total platform assets and financial advisors served. Crager and the team at Envestnet were first in the managed solutions industry to think more globally about how to streamline an independent advisor's practice by putting a broad range of fee-based products side by side in an easily accessed open-architecture portal.

The Managed Money Institute named Crager the 2015 Industry Pioneer, the organization's highest honor. Before joining Envestnet, Crager served as a managing director at Rittenhouse Financial Services. There, he developed a widely recognized initiative that integrated value-added investor communications with a technology-driven client service platform.

Crager is a frequent speaker on industry topics. He is passionate about the need for the financial services industry to increase its diversity as well as encouraging college students to graduate and enter the industry. Crager and his wife, Kathy, live in Berwyn, Pennsylvania. They are the proud parents of three daughters and a son. Crager is a graduate of Fairfield University, where he dual majored in economics and English; he currently serves on Fairfield University's Board of Trustees.

For industry insights from Crager, follow @ENVCrager on Twitter.

JAY HUMMEL, MANAGING DIRECTOR, ENVESTNET

Mr. Hummel is the managing director of Strategic Initiatives and Thought Leadership at Envestnet. Hummel leads the firm's advisor training, consulting, and content development activities. Prior to joining

Envestnet, he was the president and COO of a large RIA based in Cincinnati, Ohio. Hummel started his career in public accounting and business consulting at Deloitte where he helped manage the day-to-day operations of the worldwide services to the Procter & Gamble Co.

Hummel has been active in leadership roles on both civic and business boards, including audit committee chair and board member of Alliance Business Lending, a regional asset-based lending company, and the Cincinnati USA Regional Chamber's Agenda 360 planning board. He is the cofounder of Fuel, an incubator focused on supplying start-up grants to emerging civic leaders. Mr. Hummel is the author of *Success and Succession*, also published by Wiley, focused on helping advisory businesses navigate the difficult transition issues that arise out of a succession process.

In 2014, Hummel received the University of Cincinnati's Jeffrey Hurtwitz Award, recognizing the university's top alumnus under the age of 35. Hummel and his wife, Valerie, live in Cincinnati. They are the proud parents of two young sons, Cooper and Dylan.

For industry insights from Hummel, follow @ENVHummel on Twitter.

About the Contributors

JUD BERGMAN, CHAIRMAN AND CEO, ENVESTNET

Jud Bergman is responsible for leading the Envestnet organization, and is focused on guiding the company's strategy, as well as organizational and business development. Prior to founding Envestnet, Bergman was the managing director, Nuveen Mutual Funds, for Nuveen Investments, a diversified investment manager. In this role he was responsible for the profitable growth of Nuveen's mutual fund business and was a member of Nuveen's Investment Management Committee. From 1992 to 1997, Bergman directed Nuveen's Corporate Development activity, where he initiated the development of Nuveen's separately managed account business and helped guide the firm's expansion into a diversified investment manager beyond municipal investments.

Bergman is a frequent speaker and respected thought leader in the financial services industry. Bergman was named to the 2015 *Worth* magazine's Power 100, recognizing the 100 most powerful men and women in finance.

JEAN CHATZKY, FINANCIAL EDITOR, NBC'S *TODAY* SHOW

Jean Chatzky, the financial editor for NBC's *TODAY* show, is an award-winning personal finance journalist, AARP's personal finance ambassador and an educational partner for Fidelity. Chatzky is a best-selling author; her most recent books are *Operation Money*, a free financial guide for military service members and families; and *Money Rules: The Simple Path to Lifelong Security.* She believes knowing how to manage our money is one of the most important life skills for people at every age and has made it her mission to help simplify money matters, increasing financial literacy both now and for the future.

In 2015, Chatzky teamed up with Time for Kids and The PwC Charitable Foundation to launch *Your $*, a financial literacy magazine reaching 2 million schoolchildren each month. She lives with her family in Westchester County, New York.

PAM KRUEGER, EXECUTIVE PRODUCER, *MONEYTRACK*

Pam Krueger created the award-winning *MoneyTrack* investor-education television series seen nationally on more than 250 PBS stations. She is the recipient of a 2010 and 2009 Gracie Award and brings her knowledge and can-do attitude to viewers nationwide, educating the public about financial advisors and personal investing.

Krueger serves on the board of directors of the California Jump$tart Coalition, an organization dedicated to increasing financial literacy among children and teens, and she received the Financial Educator of the Year Award in 2010 from the Financial Literacy Institute. Krueger is now developing WealthRamp, an online matching service that brings consumers and advisors together using a systematic and educational approach.

Index

Page references in *italics* refer to figures.